Priceless Memories

A Journey back in time with a Leader
worth following

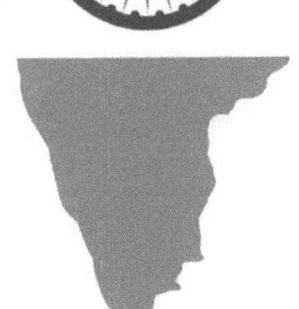

"Trust in the Lord with all thine heart; and lean unto thine own understanding. In all thy ways acknowledge Him and He shall direct thy path"

-Proverbs 3:5 & 6

by Sushila Patnaik

ARPress
ILLUMINATING IDEAS.
EMPOWERING VOICES.

ARPress
45 Dan Road Suite 5
Canton MA 02021

Hotline: 1(888) 821-0229
Fax: 1(508) 545-7580

Ordering Information:

Quantity sales. Special discounts are available on quantity purchases by corporations, associations, and others. For details, contact the publisher at the address above.

Printed in the United States of America.

ISBN-13:   Softcover   979-8-89356-926-1
                    eBook   979-8-89356-928-5
                    Hardcover   979-8-89356-927-8

Library of Congress Control Number: 2024906121

TABLE OF CONTENTS

Dedication..1

Acknowledgement...3

Prologue 5

The Beginning 7

A home built on solid rock..9

World war 2...11

Pray without ceasing..13

Celebrating christmas..16

Jesus the cornerstone 19

Theophilus...21

A shepherd and his flock..23

Tragedy strikes...25

Jehovah jireh...28

Jehovah-ropheka..30

A brother who cared...33

Hard work has its reward..36

God's plan for patricia and kumila...38

Our lord must have full control 40

God honors those who honor him 43

God turns pain into joy 46

Trained to serve 49

A silver lining behind the clouds..52

He is able to move mountains 56

A new beginning 59

God has a plan for me 62

God works in a mysterious way...65

Unexpected promotion 67

Patricia and Stuart...69

God's provision...72

From the united kingdom to the united states..75

Making a house a home..77

A garden to admire...79

The sun outside and the son inside 82

Man looks at the outward appearance but god looks at the heart.......................85

A teacher with new perspective 88

A labor of love 90

Extended family 93

A mother's heart breaks for the third time 96
The loss of a son takes its toll... 99
A dream becomes a reality.. 102
Joy turned to sorrow 107
Our greatest regret... 109
Waiting is not easy but necessary 111
The forgotten group.. 115
Our last christmas together 118
A test of true love 120
It takes courage to do what is right.. 122
Final preparation 125
Absent in the body present with the lord 127
Passing the baton... 130

Dedicated to John and Bhagyabati Patnaik (Mom and Dad)

ACKNOWLEDGEMENT

Before I even begin writing, I need to acknowledge two very special people who have played a very important part in my life without whom I would not have been able to make this journey through life.

The first and the most important is the Lord Jesus Christ who has had me in the palms of His hand from the time I was born and has never ever left my side even when I went through times when I felt alone. He has lifted me up and made me who I am and to Him be all Glory and Honor. I am looking forward to seeing Him when He takes me home.

The second person, and I know she will be shocked to hear it, is my younger sister (who is taller than all the sisters). Honestly, I owe her much and she may not realize it. She has been with me through thick and thin and has trusted me to make discussions for our family and I hope I did not let her down.

I know it was very difficult for her when I got vitiligo and my skin, especially my face, began to lose color and I became the cause of laughter, comments, and people staring at my face. She volunteered to cut my hair even though she had no experience in doing so, and may I say, did a terrific job and saved me a lot of money. Although she had never cooked in her life, she had the responsibility of cooking the meals even when she had to leave home by 5:10 a.m. I was free to take care of our mother and also got my MA while our mother was very sick and could not take care of herself.

I know I spent more time with our mother before and after work while she was in the hospital, but nobody knew that she had my meals ready and brought it with her so that she could spend time with our mother too.

It took love, guts and devotion to make those trips to work so early in the morning in public transport, cook all the three meals, and spend a few hours in the hospital and nursing home. Thank you, Rajini. You were the best and I thank you for being there with us as you gave your best in your service to the Lord. I thank God for you. May He bless you and give us many more years together.

PROLOGUE

At the very beginning, let me assure you this was not my idea! Somebody had faith in me and saw something that I was not aware of. Since my sister Patricia and her husband live "Down Under" (Australia), communication between us was limited to speaking by phone once a week. I felt encouragement was a gift I had received from God and email was such an easy way of communicating and encouraging not only them but my friends and past students who are either still in school or in college. Something in my emails (and I know it was of the Lord) caused my brother-in-law and my sister to tell me that I should write a book that others could read and be inspired by it. After much persistence and encouragement from them, I said I would think about it. Believe it or not, I finally committed this whole idea into the Lord's hands and prayed for clarity. All my life, although I worked hard and with the help of the Lord accomplished much, I felt I was no good where the world was concerned because of my stature and my looks. Now, God was giving me an opportunity to write on His behalf and find healing in my life and realize I am special to God and I am His instrument in His hands to bring glory to Him.

I am very certain it is not going to be about me but what God has achieved because of the faith and actions of two uneducated insignificant people—my parents—who lived in a time where they were considered backward and who could never achieve much. They are now with the Lord but look where we (their children) have come and what we—with the help of the Almighty God—have achieved! That is what I have always wanted to talk about.

I would like to point out that it does not matter who we are or what status we have, it is who we are in Christ and what we can achieve because of Him. I would like to uplift Christ who did it all because my parents were willing to submit to the will of Almighty God. It is my desire that this book will be an encouragement to you and draw you to the foot of the cross where you will find hope, fulfillment and rest.

The Lord has created each one of us in His image for a purpose and that is to acknowledge Him as the Lord of our lives and glorify Him in all that we do. May you have the courage to accept Him as your Savior and allow Him to direct your path. You will never regret it. Psalm 34:8 says, "Oh taste and see that the Lord is good; blessed is the man who trusts in Him."

THE BEGINNING

I wondered what went on in my mother's mind when she was barely a kid, the only girl with three brothers in the family. My maternal grandpa had gone home to be with the Lord and she was left with her siblings and her mother. She lived in a remote country at a time when women were considered only necessary to keep the fire burning, the house cleaned, and the family fed. Playing was not an option. The moment her chores were done, she was advised by her eldest brother to go into the house and read the only Bible available to them. I wonder what I would have done in a similar situation. But she in those earlier days of her life understood what it meant to obey those in authority over her. Her eldest brother was now the head of the house and the only provider. She loved reading the Bible and she did so willingly. She wanted a relationship with God who understood her needs. She knew that God would speak to her and He did. There in that little hut she came face to face with her maker and her Savior. She submitted herself to Him right there and knew she was a child of God. She knew that He had her future in His hands. He would work out the details. It reminds me of an old-time favorite song of mine and I quote, "I don't know about tomorrow, but I know who holds my hands."

Although she did not have what we consider important to us in this age of self-centeredness, she had something the "world could not give and could not take away." She had Jesus, the one who was not only there when she was born, there when her father died, and was now with her in her teenage years. He loved her and gave His life to redeem her. He had promised never to leave her nor forsake her, and He kept his promise.

As a young child, she had attended school only for a few years which in our present society is being uneducated. She was a farmer's daughter and the only trade she knew was farming. Being poor, she was fortunate if she had two changes of clothes. She was not allowed to have friends or entertainment, but she was given the best opportunity, one we take for granted, and that was to talk to her Savior and read His word and she made the best of both. In my book, she was wiser and richer than most of us. For all our education, and the treasures we have accumulated are of no use when we leave this world. We cannot take them with us. We have to meet our maker, and the only thing He is looking for is our name in the "Lamb's book of life" and that can only happen if we have submitted ourselves to Jesus, asked Him to come into our hearts, and be the Lord of our lives. Then only can we be born again into the Family of God and we are able to enjoy the home He has prepared for us.

May I ask you, my readers, a question? Is your name written in the "Lamb's Book of Life?" Have you committed your life to Jesus, and did you accept Him as your Savior? It is the most important thing you need to do. That is the only thing that matters. You will have to leave everything you have accumulated when you meet your maker and He does not recognize you as His child. Of what use was all the wealth you have, or the popularity contest you won. Nothing matters anymore. It's not too late. Accept Him now and live for Him until He calls you home.

A Home Built On Solid Rock

Dad

On his 25th birthday, as was the custom, a friend introduced my paternal grandpa and his son John to my maternal uncle. It was then when my mom Bhagyabati and John, my father, were introduced to each other for the first time. They were engaged, and after a few months my parents were married on the 28th of December, 1935. (Can you imagine a 15-year-old girl from one of the remote country sides of Orissa, a state on the east coast of India, leaving home with someone she had known only for a few months?)

They travelled by train to live with my dad and his family in the populous city of Calcutta where people spoke three different languages. None of these languages included Oriya, which was what they spoke in her hometown. The people in her neighborhood practiced different religions. In our minds that was disastrous, but not in the mind of our Creator, God. My parents both loved and worshiped the Almighty God. They had committed their lives to Him. He was in control and He would remove all barriers and bring harmony.

This was a very difficult situation. But we as believers must remember that God does not promise us a rose garden without any thorns but He does promise us that He will never leave us alone nor forsake us. Proverbs 3:6 says, *"In all thy ways acknowledge Him and He shall direct thy path."* This is a promise from God that He will lead us and I know He will not fail us. Blessed be His name! Does that encourage you to commit unto the Lord and allow Him to direct your path? I hope it does. You will never regret it.

My parents had two important things in common. They knew, loved, and worshiped the Almighty God and they spoke the same language. That was enough to begin their new life together. Life in this new environment wasn't easy. At the age of 15, Mom was responsible for running a household of seven, including her in-laws and their three young children. It was more than a full-time job with no one to guide or assist her except our Heavenly Father. Mom depended on His love, guidance, and protection and spent much time seeking His help. It must have been a difficult task, but with the help of the Lord she was able to begin every new day with more strength and confidence that God would see her through. Unfortunately, my father was away all day at work, "bringing home the bacon" that would keep the family provide for. Dad used to leave very early in the morning for work and got home very late after work. Though they spent very little time together, Mom knew Dad loved and respected her. He had confidence that everything in the Homefront would be taken care of even when he was away from home.

Meanwhile, our family had grown. We now had three brothers: Theophilus, Zechariah, and Obadiah. Although it seemed a long time coming, Dad finally had the courage to move his wife and children to a new home. During those years, Mom had not only drawn closer to the Lord, but had taught herself to read and write Hindi, the national language, and Bengali, the state language.

My parents asked God to provide a good English Christian school for their three sons. They had great faith that God would not only provide a school, but their boys were going to attend the best British school in town. (This was a tall order but my parents knew it was a possibility with God.) They prayed fervently and knew that God would grant it if it was according to His will.

WORLD WAR 2

1944 was a difficult year for everyone. World War 2 was in progress. Patricia, the fourth child, was about to be born. Living in Calcutta was dangerous due to the war. In order to keep Mom and the children safe, Dad sent them back to her hometown to live with her brothers and mom. Since her hometown was in a remote area, it was safer than living in the city of Calcutta which was the major hub of India. Just imagine—Mom pregnant with my sister, with three young boys to take care of and away from her home. There was no communication between my parents during that time because the only way to communicate was by mail, which was not a priority. Everyone in that countryside convinced our mother that something had gone wrong. She needed to be prepared for the worst. But not so for Mom. She refused to listen to them and continued to trust God to bring Dad home to her and their children. She was rewarded for her implicit faith. The war finally came to an end although no one heard this good news in Mandapara where Mom and the three boys were living.

Then early one morning, while the boys were playing outside, one of their neighbors spotted my dad walking towards the house calling for the boys who were still playing in the dirt. The boys were so excited to see Dad that they all ran to get the attention they deserved. The neighbors ran to tell our mother the good news. Mom stood in disbelief, but when she saw Dad at the door, she wept tears of joy and just thanked God for answering her prayers. What a reunion! Dad not only had Mom and the three boys, but for the first time met his little girl, Patricia. What a reward for a life of faith? I was amazed when I heard the story for the first time. Not only was the war over but everyone was safe and once again reunited and they could return to their home in Calcutta. This was God's doing. My parents had put their total trust in God and He was not going to let them down.

God can do the same for you in situations that seem very difficult to understand. But He must have your total dependence on Him. Will you take a step of faith and give your life totally to Christ? I can assure you that He considers you precious and the Bible confirms that He will never ever let you down.

Unknown to our mother, Dad had been working with a serious injury to his ankle. During the war, when a fighter jet is seen in the sky, there is a siren and immediately there is a total blackout. Dad was on his way home after a hard day's work during one of these blackouts. He did not see the ditch and fell into it and broke his ankle. He took care of it but because he could not take sick leave, he continued to stand on his feet all day as he cooked for a lot of people. The ankle finally healed, but the pressure of standing on his feet damaged his right knee and for the rest of his life had to take injections to eradicate the pain. But Dad just continued to do his job to the best of his ability until the Lord took him home.

PRAY WITHOUT CEASING

Dad and Mom continued to pray that the Lord would provide a good English Christian school for my brothers. They had great faith and went to meet the principal of the most prestigious school in Calcutta, which was only for the elite. Dad did not have the money to pay for tuition and the boys did not speak or read English. But my parents had faith and continued to pray that somehow a miracle would happen and the boys could go to Calcutta Boys School.

At first, they were rejected, but my parents kept praying and waited on the Lord. Much to Dad's surprise, he had a special visit from one of the teachers at the Calcutta Boys School several days later. Dad was informed that Mr. Hicks, the principal of the Calcutta Boys School, wanted to meet with Dad and the three boys the next day. My parents could not wait to thank God. The next day, Dad took the three boys, dressed in their Sunday best, to meet the principal. Somehow Mr. Hicks had found a scholarship to pay all of the tuition for the three boys. The only condition was that the boys would have to catch up with their individual assignments, pass the examination at the end of the school year if they wished to continue in that school.

Even though this seemed impossible, to my parents it was a possibility. They knew they had God on their side. They could not afford to have the boys tutored, but each of them had teachers who loved teaching and worked with the boys during the school hours to help them succeed. My brothers were excited to be in a prestigious school and did their best to complete their assignments. My parents continued to pray for the boys. The teachers did not give up and continued to give their very best. With the help of God, the boys were able to graduate to the next class.

I am reminded of a chorus I learned in my younger years. It goes like this, *"Got any rivers you think are uncrossable, got any mountains you can't tunnel through? God specializes in things deemed impossible. He can do when nothing else will do."* Take heart my friend, *"He is able to do exceedingly, abundantly above all that we ask or think, according to the powers that worketh in us,"* Ephesians 3:21.

I think the best part of being in that particular school was that it was not only a school with high educational standards but it was a Christian school. From a very early age the boys were taught the Bible and the standard of living the Lord expected of them. They produced the best plays and concerts, and they were given every opportunity to develop extracurricular activities like sports.

While the boys were still in school, my parents were gifted with three more girls after Patricia. I was the second, followed by Kumila and Rajini. My parents were determined to put the girls into an English-speaking Christian school, but it had to be nearby, so Mom could walk us back and forth from school.

God is good and gave us the opportunity to attend Welland Gouldsmith School. It was not a big or renowned school, but one that was suitable for us. We were happy because the students were mostly from our neighborhood. We loved it and enjoyed the friendship of our peers. We had to wear uniforms just like our brothers did, and the discipline and the teaching were good. We had a very small playground, but the children were happy to be there and enjoyed every moment of their time in school. The school prepared the children for high school and later for Senior Cambridge.

We participated in inter school sports, basketball, and choir. Going to a Christian school in Calcutta for boys and girls was very demanding. In early elementary class, we had to learn to read and write three languages and pass in every subject before we were promoted to the next grade. English became our first language in school even though some children did not know a word of English. Indian children were expected to speak their Indian language at home. It was difficult for us to learn three languages while we were still very young. But children who attended English- speaking schools counted it a privilege to have the opportunity to do so. They did their best, not only to pass the examinations but to do well because of the opportunities that were available to them when they graduated.

We knew our parents wanted us to be successful in school so that we could venture out into the world and follow our calling. They wanted us to break the barriers that had been created by society, where girls were called to be wives and mothers, and boys were expected to follow in their father's footsteps. They wanted to prove that if we were in the center of God's will, then He would help us break this barrier and accomplish anything God had planned for us, but we had to do our best.

I think my mom had the most difficult task. She not only took care of the home, but us also. She made sure our uniforms were washed and ironed every day because it was very humid in Calcutta. Each morning our teachers checked us for cleanliness before we entered the classroom. They used to say, "Cleanliness is next to Godliness." Each day after we left home for school, Mom would prepare a three-course lunch for us. Then she would put it in containers with plates and utensils and send it by hired hand to our respective schools. She had to have lunch ready by 11.00 a.m. We were the envy of our fellow students when we opened our lunch boxes. You see, our parents believed "A healthy body would have a healthy mind." After the lunch was picked up, she would wash each garment by hand and dry the clothes on a line outside. Before she could take a break, she would heat the iron (which was a solid piece of heavy iron with a handle on it) on a coal fire. She had to clean the iron to remove rust stains. Then she ironed seven sets of uniforms and Dad's working clothes and got it ready for the next day. Then only she could relax and have her lunch.

We are so spoiled with a washing machine, dryer, and a dishwasher. I can't imagine living a life without it. I think my parents worked hard and expected high standards from themselves because in doing so, they taught us that hard work never killed a person but produced good results. By their example they made us realize the integrity of a job well done. They had us believe that God expected nothing but the best from us, and in so doing we were blessed because we pleased God. They did not expect more from us than they were willing to give. As a result, we not only appreciated what they did but let it influence us in the way we treated any assignments that were given to us.

Remember parents, that it is not what you say to your child, but how you say it and model it, that will leave an impression on your child which they will never forget and they will always strive to attain.

While taking care of the home and family, which was more than a full- time job, Mom found ways and means to supplement Dad's income. Again, it was hard work. She bought bags of tomatoes and eggplants when they were in season and the price was good. She was an exceptional cook in her own right. She made bottles of delicious hot Indian pickles. This was a tedious job. Then she would carry it to those who had placed an order and sell it at a reasonable price. (You should have seen her face when she brought the cash home! She was able to buy things her family needed and that gave her great joy.)

CELEBRATING CHRISTMAS

Two weeks before Christmas, all the children in our family went carol singing with the church. It was instilled in us that Christmas was a time to share the good news with the community around us. So we met at the church every day at about 6 p.m. and piled into a bus. During these two weeks, we visited nursing homes, high-rise apartment buildings, restaurants, children's hospitals and sang a few carols at each of the places we stopped at. The leader of our group made sure the people who listened to us singing heard about what Christmas was all about and the reason we were there. We had a lot of fun as we sang and shared the Christmas message. The donations we collected were used to send the boarding children in the Welland Gouldsmith School to camp during a week in summer.

These children were very special. Many of these children did not have a family or a home to live in. They spent their entire life at the school until they graduated. So our effort during the two weeks not only allowed us to spread the Christmas message and have a lot of fun and enjoyment, but it also enabled us to give these children a special time of fun and relaxation away from boarding school. Carol singing was a three-fold blessing. It was a great blessing to us as we shared. It was a blessing to the people we shared the message with. The children who knew nothing of the joys of living with their family were blessed with a wonderful vacation.

Christmas was also a very special occasion in our family. You see, we lived among people who did not know Christ as we did. So, our parents taught us when we were still very young that Christmas was a time of giving. "God gave His only son for our redemption." So, if we wanted to celebrate Christmas, we had to give our best to those who did not know Him.

When Mom was still young, she had learned to make a lot of goodies out of rice flour and she had learned to bake a Christmas cake from Dad. So that was what we had to do. Our celebration began weeks before Christmas. I still remember the girls had to help Mom pound many kilos of rice into flour and then strain it in a sieve to make sure it was smooth. We had to cut very finely many pounds of a variety of dried fruits and nuts. A few days before Christmas, Mom hired a baker because we did not have an oven and two large deep bowls to whip up the egg whites and the batter for about 40 pounds of cake. Mom personally supervised the whole process. We eagerly watched as the batter was made with the eggs, butter, sugar, flour etc. and all the fruits and nuts were added and then poured into rectangular pans. Mom had our names written on the outside of the pans. She counted all the pans and then went with the baker to his bakery and waited while the cakes baked. When it was ready, she brought them home, let them cool, and put them into containers.

During the next several days, Pat and I helped her make various kinds of goodies using rice flour and the all-purpose flour, eggs, and sugar. Two days before Christmas, Patricia and I took trays of those goodies and fruits and distributed them to all our neighbors, most of whom were non-Christians. We always wished them a Merry Christmas. They were surprised and considered themselves very fortunate to be remembered in such a special way on the most important day in our Christian calendar.

This may seem strange to you, but it was what our parents taught us to remind us what Christmas was all about. It was about God showing us the height and depth of His love for us. John 3: 16 says, and I quote, *"For God so loved the world that he gave his only begotten son, that whosoever believeth in Him should not perish but have everlasting life."* Christmas was a time when God's son Jesus left his heavenly home and was born in a manger. He spent three years of his adult life teaching people the way, the truth, and life. He performed many miracles, healed the sick, raised the dead, and ultimately sacrificed His life to bring redemption for man. This was not easy, but because of His sacrifice we can, if we believe and accept Him as our Savior, we will inherit eternal life. He gave the greatest gift of all. We in turn must give and share that precious gift with others.

Christmas was not about what we could get. It was about sharing with others that great news. I think the world would have us believe that Christmas was a time to wear new clothes, go to parties, get a lot of presents, and for the business people a time to make money. Christ whose birthday we were celebrating is nowhere in the picture. But to us kids, giving to others and sharing the message of Christmas was part of our Christmas tradition. It left a very special memory in our lives, one we will never forget and one we hope to continue on a smaller scale as long as we live.

As I look back to the way we celebrated Christmas, I can honestly say that my parents in their simple way had taught us the "True Meaning of Christmas." It was not how much we could get but to give because we had received the most precious gift even when we did not deserve it.

JESUS THE CORNERSTONE

The most important part of the day for my parents was spending time with their Heavenly Father. I still remember my parents waking up early in the morning to spend time with God. Even though Dad had a bad knee, he read his Bible and then on bended knees he prayed for himself and his family. He prayed that God would protect us, provide for us, and lead us throughout the day. Then he would wake us before he left for work at 6:15 in the morning. We had breakfast, dressed, then walked to school. When we returned from school, we changed into our house clothes, and ate the snack mom had prepared for us. After Patricia and I had cleaned the lantern (because we had no electricity), we got to play for a while. Exactly at 5 p.m., Mom put the mat down and the six children sat around the mat (Theo was in boarding school at Calcutta Boys school) and took out their books and homework. The older kids had to help the younger kids if we had a problem. Mom sat on a stool outside the circle watching carefully to make sure we were doing what we were supposed to do. We could not say we had no homework. We had to occupy ourselves, learning our times table, spelling words, working on some math problem, or reading a book. We had to sit there for at least two hours. Then we got to play for a short time while we waited for Dad to come home, which was after 8 p.m.

We were tired and hungry, but excited to see him. It was past eight and we were ready for dinner, but Dad would say, "No dinner until devotion." He really believed that "the family that prays together, stays together." Where my mom and dad were concerned, Christ was the head of the house and He deserved the first place. We sat in a circle on the mat and sang a song. Dad read the Bible and prayed. We did not know how to read in our native language, but we could understand everything. However, waiting for prayer to be over was difficult for Pat and me. I still remember, Pat and I would be almost asleep when we heard the family recite the Lord's Prayer together after Dad had prayed. Immediately, we nudged each other and took part in the prayer.

This may seem strange to you, but it left a permanent mark in my life. It made me understand that to my parents, God was the most important person, one who had to be revered and obeyed. It taught me, too, that the Bible was the living word of God wherein God gave instructions for our daily living. It also instilled in me that no matter what we did, "without God we were nothing, but with God we were more than conquerors in Christ Jesus." What a lesson to learn at such an early age! The Bible, as soon as I was able to get an English translation, became an integral part of my life.

After family prayers, we children had our dinner. Dad always asked Mom to cook for two extra people, in case we had a visitor. Our home was always open to a missionary passing through, a stranger who was hungry or a visitor. They shared our meal and sometimes spent the night at our home. My parents made sure there was enough for the children and visitors before they sat down to eat.

While the rest of the children had leisure time after dinner, Pat and I had to scrub all the brass utensils. Dad made sure we understood that Mom was not a servant. She took care of everything while we got to enjoy school and play. So, when we were home, it was our duty to clean up. You may think that Dad was mean, but that was not true. He had explained to us that we could be anything we wanted to be with our education, but we would always have to make our house a home. We had to learn the skills that made a good home. I know that Dad and Mom trained us early in life to be good home-makers.

I know the children of today would be surprised to learn that we kids were very happy in the environment we grew up in, but we were. We had learned a few important lessons while we were very young.

Having parents who loved and served God was a treasure to have. Being a part of a family where parents loved you was a beautiful gift.

We were taught the values of life which were to love God and your family, honor and appreciate your parents.

Money does not bring joy but provides the necessities of life. Be content with what you have and make the best of it.

Do your best and aim high.

So, we grew up missing nothing and enjoying the simple things of life and we were happy.

THEOPHILUS

From the time he was in high school, Theo, as he was called, not only studied in Calcutta Boys School but lived there. I think the principal saw the potential in him and realized that living in school would give him the opportunity to cultivate his potential to the maximum capacity, and it did. He not only became an exceptional student but developed his musical skills as well as other extracurricular activities. He learned to read music, play the trumpet and the piano.

After he had graduated with his senior Cambridge, Theo decided to get his B.A. from the Calcutta Bible College that had been established by the Carey Baptist Church. He also enrolled to get his bachelor's degree at the University of Calcutta. It was tough, but he thought it was a good way to make the best use of the time available to him. So, he went to Bible College during the day and the secular college during the evening. I do not know when he studied, but he did well in both the schools.

Almost everyone at the university was a non-Christian. This was different from the Christian atmosphere he was used to, but it did not stop him from enjoying his time there. He was friendly with all the men in his class but maintained his walk with the Lord. He was true to Him and took a stand for Him without being offensive. One incident comes to my mind. Almost everyone smoked in the evening college and had tried to get Theo to do so. Instead of saying it was wrong, he told them he would use a trashcan to get rid of excess paper but not burn it in his mouth. The students got the point and respected him for that. I will never forget how proud I was of him when he told us that story. I guess being a Christian is living it. I am sure those non-Christian friends were amazed, because they never ever asked him to smoke a cigarette again.

Why am I taking the time to give such details? It is not to prove to you that my brother was exceptional and never made a mistake. I am sure he did, but he knew he belonged to Christ and had to take a stand for Him even at a college where there were no Christian friends or family. It was important to show what living a Christian life was all about shining a torch for a Savior who had given His life for us. So even though we lived in the world, we were not of the world. Our lives belong to Christ and we must represent Him wherever we are. It is not easy, but with Christ as our leader we can accomplish the mission.

A SHEPHERD AND HIS FLOCK

By this time Theo had been attending the Carey Baptist Church where he became very close to the pastor and his wife. They were sent by their home church in England to be a pastor in the church we attended. This church was started by William Carey, the founder of the modern missionary. Pastor and Mrs. Collette had not only volunteered to preach to the congregation but they truly believed they were called to be a shepherd to their flock. About 50-60% of those who attended the church were students, most of whom came from the hill tribes of Assam, Darjeeling and Nagaland, Burma and Andaman Island. They attended either the Calcutta Bible College or secular and medical schools. Most of these students were away from home. Some of the students who went to local schools were non-Christians and attended the church. Pastor and Mrs. Collette were true to their calling and became part of their lives. Pastor Collette spent much time with the young men and boys while Mrs. Collette took the young women and girls under her care. Their home was always open to the students, and they were available whenever and wherever they were needed.

Pastor Collette never returned to his home in England. Calcutta had become their home and the students were part of his family, and he ministered in the Carey Baptist Church until he died and went home to be with his maker. As part of their ministry, they shared their home, gave guidance, preached, and encouraged the members of his congregation. Though he came from England, he spoke Hindi fluently. Even though we had a Pastor for the Hindi-speaking congregation, he sometimes ministered to the Hindi speaking congregation too.

Rev. Collette took Theo under his wings. Pastor was an excellent pianist and he taught Theo how to play the piano better. He also let Theo practice his trumpet as he accompanied him on the piano. Theo became an accomplished trumpet player and sometimes played for the church worship service. I think Carey Baptist Church was a place where he not only became a confident trumpet player but where he decided to join full-time ministry. Many of the students from Nagaland who attended the church also decided to go back to their state as full-time Bible teachers, missionaries, and Pastors.

Theo spent much of his free time with Pastor Collette, who realized that Theo had the potential to make a fine preacher. Pastor spoke to a friend of his in America who was willing to sponsor him. This would enable Theo to further his education in biblical studies. Theo discussed it with Dad. Dad and Mother had prayed for this opportunity, but now that the time had come, it was difficult for them to let their son go. Theo had been working as a schoolteacher at the Calcutta Boys School. He was taking care of his own board and lodging, as well as helping with expenses at home. The family needed this extra help, and Dad could have said no. But my parents knew they had prayed for their children and this was of the Lord. They loved the Lord and He would provide for Theo in America as well as provide for the rest of the family at home. So, both of them gave their blessings to this new venture and prayed for God to work it out according to His will.

TRAGEDY STRIKES

When I finished eight grade, I was accepted into Pratt Memorial School (a very prestigious school) for high school. The school was very far from home, but it was worth it. It was a huge facility with a big playground. It was a school for the elite, and I felt like a fish out of water. The distance from home gave me very little time to do my homework, but I used every opportunity to do the best I could. Somehow I got through the first two years of high school, which was very interesting. Our principal believed in hands-on learning, and we visited several places where we were given not only a tour but practical training. On one occasion, we went to a steel manufacturing factory which was many miles away from home. These trips were exciting, and we learned a lot from those experiences.

Zachariah and Obediah had both graduated from school and completed Senior Cambridge. They were ready to begin a new chapter in their lives. Pat had finished with Welland Gouldsmith School and decided to go for training to be a stenographer. I was in eleventh grade as we call it in India, and Kumila and Rajini were still in Welland Gouldsmith School, when tragedy struck our family.

Dad was the only working member in our home. He sometimes worked ten hours in the day. He was never sick, but one day came home very sick. He was never known to lie down when it was time to be at work. Something had happened. The doctor was called. She checked him out thoroughly and gave him medicine. She hoped he would be up in a day or two. But instead of getting better, Dad got worse. Theo consulted with Mr. Hicks who was still the principal of Calcutta Boys School. He recommended he should take Dad to the R G Kar Hospital, which was one of the best hospitals in town. Mr. Hicks knew the senior doctor. Dad was quickly taken to the hospital, where he received immediate attention. It was a Sunday, and both Theo and Mom came home, reassured he was doing better.

On Monday, when we came home from school, we heard Dad was not doing too well. Theo and Mom stayed with him, while the rest of the family waited patiently. Around 1:00 a.m. in the morning, we heard a knock. Everyone was awake, eager to hear the latest news. We saw Theo with his arms around Mom who was weeping her heart out. We knew it was bad news. Theo explained to us that Dad had a massive heart attack and had gone home to meet his Savior. How could this happen? How could God do such a thing to a person who loved and served Him all his life? Didn't He know there were still six children depending on him? Dad was the only breadwinner in the house. What would happen to the family now? I am sure each one of us had many questions in our hearts, but there was no time to ponder these questions that bothered us. We sat there not knowing what would happen next.

For the first time, we saw utter despair in our mother's face. She'd lost the love of her life and there was nothing she could do. She had never been to a funeral, but she knew that much had to be done. We lived among people who were either Hindus, Muslims, or Buddhist. Even though they would have loved to help, they knew nothing about Christian burials.

Theo immediately stepped in. He did not know what to do, but he assured our mother he'd take care of the situation. None of us thought of breakfast that day. We knew that Dad's body would be brought home and we waited for its arrival. I still remember my youngest sister waiting on the balcony saying, "Daddy is coming," when they brought the casket to our home. She did not understand what death was. She was the baby in the house, and everyone treated her as such. I wondered what went on in her mind when she saw the body lying on the bed, without movement or response.

After Dad's body was brought home and laid on the bed, Theo went to make arrangements for the burial. The first thing was to find a burial spot, but when he went to the cemetery, he found it to be full, and the next one was outside the city many, many miles away. He was dejected and did not know what to do and what to tell Mom. As he walked home to give Mom the bad news, he met with a friend who asked Theo why he was so sad. Theo explained the situation. He told his friend he could not face Mom with the news. To his surprise, his friend had an answer which he felt would solve Theo's problem. He had a plot already purchased and was willing to sell it to Theo for a very small amount. Theo couldn't believe it. Our God is amazing! He always knows our needs before we even ask Him for His help. This was no accident. It was God's provision for His child. Theo, for the first time in his life, did not know what to say. He accepted his friend's proposal and came home to give our mother the good news. Mom knew God would intervene and she could depend on Him.

With the help of Pastor Collette and Mr. Hicks, Theo made the funeral arrangements. Except for a few cars, most of the people walked behind the casket even though the cemetery was very far from home. It was a grand procession made up of neighbors, friends, and people who had been helped by my father. It was a sight to behold. I will never forget it. I could not believe that my father was loved and respected by so many people, most of whom were non-Christians. They had come to pay their last respects. Later we learned that most of the people who had come considered Dad to be a special friend who treated the people kindly and who was always there when they needed help. To Dad, everyone he came in contact with was a person created by God and deserved to be treated with respect.

On his tomb is a cross with the words, *"Precious in the sight of the Lord is the death of his saints,"* Psalm 115:16. Indeed, to the One who loved Dad and gave His life for him, Dad was precious and he was going home.

*J*EHOVAH *J*IREH

Now the seven children who had looked up to Dad not only because he was the head of the house but because of the leadership and example he had set for his family were without the provider. Although he had earned a meager wage, he had taught us that anything placed in the hands of God could be multiplied as were the loaves and fishes which fed the 5,000.Dad had taught us that it was not who we were in society or how much we earned that mattered. It was what we placed in the Master's hand that made the difference. God requires the first fruits of what we have before we start to spend it. What a valuable lesson we had the privilege of learning!

I still remember Dad bringing his paycheck on the last day of every month and giving it to Mom. I still remember her taking the money and placing it in front of her whilst she prayed and asked God to bless it so she could provide for her family. I remember one of the children asking for something needed for school when Dad gave her the money. She said, "You can't have it today. I need to give it first to God. Tomorrow you will get what you need." No wonder, we as kids never knew what it was to be without food, went to good schools, and dressed reasonably well. Our all- sufficient God was able to multiply what Mom had placed before Him to meet all our needs. (Remember, I said needs and not wants.)

However, we no longer had a dad or his paycheck. Some of the people in the community said, "What is going to happen now that their dad is gone? How are they going to survive? Will they still be going to Christian schools?" I do not blame them for saying this. They did not know our Heavenly Father, the One who had created this world and everything in it. The One who had promised, "Lo, I am with you always, even to the end of the world." He keeps His promise even when the situation looks bleak. But would our faith survive this test?

Mom was prepared to go to work as a maid or a housekeeper. But my brothers would have none of it. They knew Dad would have never permitted Mom to go to work. She was his wife, the mother of his children, the one who was his soul-mate. My brothers knew that could never happen. They would share the load instead.

Zac experimented with starting a business of his own. He had his successes and his failures, but he continued to get better at it. Unfortunately, some took advantage of his youth, but he did not let that disappoint him. He continued to work hard at it and became known as a tough, smart, and successful businessman. Obe took on a full-time teaching job as well as working at his BA through the University of Calcutta in the evening. It was difficult for him and he got little sleep. Theo on the other hand continued to work in Calcutta Boys School. God was there for us, and Mom was able to keep the home fires burning. Pat took her Pitman's Shorthand seriously with the intention that she too would be able to contribute and help out the family.

A few months passed as each one of us tried to adjust to life without Dad. Theo heard from the USA. The university had accepted him, and a sponsor was willing to sign his papers on the dotted line. It should have made Theo very happy. He wanted to go and further his studies, but he also knew that now Dad was gone. He as the eldest child needed to take on the responsibility of being head of the house and also the provider.

He considered forgetting the whole idea. Mom, however, thanked God that her prayers had been answered. She knew it meant less money available for the family, but she also knew that if God had opened the door, she would not stand in the way. So, when Theo told her that he had decided not to go, she immediately told him to go with her blessing. She made sure he understood that Dad would have wanted it and God had opened the door for him. This wasn't easy for her to say. She had just buried her husband and now she would lose her eldest son. But where my mom was concerned, the welfare of her children always came first. This is what they had worked hard and prayed for and nothing would prevent it.

So, in August of that year, Theo left for the USA to begin his new life and fulfill God's purpose. It wasn't going to be easy, but he knew that with the help of the Lord and hard work he would be able to accomplish any task given to him.

JEHOVAH-ROPHEKA

Theo was gone and there was no way to make contact. Postage was expensive, and Mom couldn't write in English. The rest of the children were busy doing what they needed to do. Since each one of us had to depend on public transportation to take us from A to B, we spent much of our time riding the bus and walking to reach our destination. Mom was spending more and more time on her own. She continued to read the Bible and talk to her Heavenly Father. She would get up at 4 a.m. and pray for the children before they went to their respective school, college, or work. She worked hard to make sure the children were fed and able to do their task. She became very lonely and missed the presence of Dad in her life. She did not want to burden us with her pain. One day we suddenly realized that Mom was not her normal self. She just sat and contemplated. She was not aware of anything around her including her children. We were worried. After consultation with a doctor, we realized she had had a nervous break- down. We could not take care of her as well as do what we needed to do. Finally, Zachariah, the second eldest among the children, found a hospital back in Orissa, a city close to Mother's hometown but hundreds of miles from our home. The doctors in the hospital could treat her, but she had to be admitted into that hospital. It was very expensive. Zac volunteered to work at two jobs to pay for her medical needs. He would also pay for Kumila and Rajini, the two youngest sisters, to stay with relatives close by so they could visit and be informed of Mom's treatment.

Our family was separated, but once again we determined in our hearts to do all we could to get Mom back. So, Zac took Kumila and Rajini and Mom to Orissa. Pat and I stayed back to keep the household going. When Zac came back, he continued to work hard and returned home only to go to bed. Obe also worked hard and continued to go to evening college. Life had to go on, and no matter what the situation was, with God's help we had to continue to do our best.

Once again God intervened. The senior doctor in that hospital was a young man who knew Mom. You see, when he was a boy going to school and Mom was living with her family close by, she would help him get ready for school. This doctor had not seen her in years because Mom had married and moved to Calcutta. He was now a successful doctor and had never had the opportunity to thank Mom for all her help. God was giving him a chance to do so now. He vowed he would do his very best to make sure Mom returned home to her family fully restored. Of course, Mom did not recognize him. She did not even remember the children she loved and had been separated from. But our Almighty God knew. He understood the pain and separation the family was going through and He had planned early recovery for mom.

With God's intervention, and the doctor's hard work, Mom finally recovered after a few weeks of treatment. The first person she saw and recognized was the young doctor. She was amazed to see him after about thirty years when she had moved to Calcutta with Dad. She wondered where she was and what she was doing without her children near her. It was then that she learned she had spent several weeks in the hospital after she had had a nervous break-down. She wept her heart out and wanted to see her children. Imagine her joy when she saw Kumila and Rajini. She wanted to go home and she did. Zac immediately left home when he received the telegram and joyfully brought Mom and our two sisters home. What a reunion for the family! We had a mom and she had her children. She kissed each one with tears of joy and vowed she would never be separated from us. She was back, fully in charge, ready to cook, clean, and encourage each one of us.

This chapter in our lives was a reminder to me that we are in this world for several purposes. One of which was to remember that we get opportunities every day to be of service to someone who might be a family member, a neighbor, a co-worker, or a person we might meet for the first time. As a child of God, we are required to be sensitive to the needs around us. Ask the Lord how you might be able to help that particular person. You may be the only one who is able to help. Never do it because you expect a return favor. The Lord is aware of each individual need and might find someone else to help in your time of need or take care of it in a miraculous way.

As a young girl, Mother was advised by her brother to occupy herself, and she used her extra time to help a neighbor who had to get her children ready for school. Years later, the Lord placed this doctor, who had been helped by Mom, to treat Mom and enable her to return to her family. People may forget to reciprocate a good deed done to them, but the Lord remembers and brings help just at the right time when you might be in need of help.

May I ask you a question? Are you going through a very difficult time and you think you can't survive? Do you wonder how a Loving God could do such a thing to one of His children? Are you disheartened and feel all alone?

Take heart, my friend! How do you think we as children felt going through this difficult time? The youngest two in the family had to leave home, give up school and friends, and live with people who were almost strangers with a different way of living. Think what it meant for Zac to work at two jobs and have no time for a proper meal. On the other hand, Obediah was far from home, working hard to supplement the income and attending full-time college. Just imagine two teenagers, Patricia and me, doing what we needed to do to take care of our home, prepare food, and do our own assignments.

Had God deserted us? Indeed, He had not. He was there all the time even when we felt alone. He was proving once again that He was in control and He had a plan. He would always keep His promise if we trusted Him.

Can you trust the Lord to take you through this difficult time you might be going through? He will see you through just as He has promised. But you have to lean on Him and trust Him in every situation.

A Brother Who Cared

The experience Mom went through strengthened her spirit, and she was ready to let the Lord lead her. In turn, she was ready to take the family into a new chapter in our lives. She missed Dad, but she drew closer to the Lord. He would help her to take care of the family and continue to do what needed to be done.

The rest of us were still adjusting to the void in our lives. Zac was working in Evangelical Literature Depot as well doing a small business on the side. Pat had joined the local Youth for Christ Office to help with the secretarial work. Rajini and Urmila were continuing their schooling in Welland Gouldsmith School. Everything was going as planned. Not so for me. My life was in turmoil.

Unknown to the rest of the family, I was going through a season of despair. To me, Dad had been a man who had given his best to God and his family. He loved God and served Him in every way possible. How then could this loving God take away the one who loved Him with all his heart? Didn't He know there were seven children who needed a father? I began to question Him. I lost my faith in Him and I vowed I had had enough of Church and school. So, one day, unknown to my family, I packed up all my things in school, came home, and said I would never go back to school or church again. I know I was a big disappointment to my family, but no one said a word. I know they were concerned and prayed for me. I stayed home and helped my mother. You see, I did not actually have a relationship with God. I went to Sunday school and church and said I loved God because I wanted to please my dad. But now that he was gone, I had no need of Him.

Obediah was very hurt when he came home one day and heard I had given up church and school. Since his workplace was outside the city and he had a full-time teaching job plus full-time college, he normally stayed at the school. He was an excellent schoolteacher. He had a way with children that very few teachers had and he loved God and his family. He came to me one day with a suggestion. He had heard of a private school close to home which trained kids to finish high school at their own speed. He suggested that instead of sitting at home, I should give it a try. "No pressure," he said. "See If you can challenge yourself, and have fun."

I think I was getting bored at home without any friends, so I gave in to him. He took care of the paperwork and payment. All I had to do was enjoy it, which I did! I enjoyed it so much that I took the challenge seriously and graduated from school before my 17th birthday. I may not have had a father to encourage and motivate me, but I had a brother who cared enough to bring me back to my senses. Being part of a family that loved and cared was a very precious gift. It meant praying, sharing, and caring instead of being judgmental and nasty.

Now I understand why those children in Obediah's class loved and respected him so much. God used my brother to get me out of the rut and have a fresh beginning, but it meant that I had to listen to someone who loved God and loved me. God always has a plan for each of our lives, and the Bible says His plan is for our good. Too often, we are so engrossed in thinking about how we have been wronged or how God has let us down that we rebel and pay little attention to what God has in store for us. We can't see the big picture but He can.

There is another lesson we can learn from this. God wants us to know that we are part of a large family He created. As a member of God's family and the family we were born into, it is our responsibility to be available to care for one another. We need to be there for the one who might be hurting and tell them we care and we are there for them. Pray with them and allow God to help us minister to them. We might be the reason for that person not only to find peace but submit their life to the "Prince of Peace."

We must also remember that the best thing for us to do when we feel let down is not to fight God but let Him take over our life and future. He continues to love us even when we feel alone and He has an answer for the loneliness, rejection, or the pain we are going through.

Meanwhile, Pat had a fantastic job working as a secretary at Union Carbide, a well-known U.S. company that expected much from their workers and paid them well. Pat has a wonderful personality. She enjoyed her work and the people who worked with her. She was a good worker and always found something to laugh about. Soon she made great strides in the company and took on more responsibilities and more money than she had ever dreamed of. Her paycheck was a big asset to the family's finances and we were able to move into a bigger place.

(Do you see how God was working even though we had lost dad and my eldest brother had moved to the USA? The Bible reminds us that God will never leave the widow and the fatherless to fend for themselves. He will take the place of a father if we let Him. He works through His children and becomes their provider. He gives us able bodies and opportunities to excel if we depend upon Him and allow Him to do what seems impossible.)

HARD WORK HAS ITS REWARD

Theo in the meantime labored hard at anything he could turn his hand to. Most of the time he helped construction workers in various jobs. As a result, he became good at putting up roofs, painting, plumbing etc. He also learned to help mechanics in the car garage. It was hard work but it paid for his board, lodging, and college. He excelled at school and finished both his Master's. He found a good job and was able to provide for himself. He was a good preacher and was loved by those he ministered to. He married Sonia, and together they set up home. They had a beautiful home and had two beautiful girls, Monica and Christina.

Zac also found the love of his life. His wife's name was Conica who had finished Bible College and was a very good pianist. They lived in a beautiful home a few miles away from our apartment. They had two children. Rajiv was the firstborn and Ritika was born ten years later. When the children were much older, they moved to the USA and lived in Redding, California where both children went to school and Conica got her Master's degree.

Obe graduated from the University of Calcutta with a B.A. degree. He had a good job, but knew that God had something special for him to do. He must have consulted with Theo, who in turn felt he could sponsor him if he chose to study in the USA. After much prayer, Obe decided to take the opportunity to further his education in America. This was a hard blow for Mom, but with a smiling face, she told Obe to go with her blessing. Within a few months, the paperwork was taken care of, and we as a family said good-bye to him.

He had been accepted by the Golden Gate Seminary. I think it was the same one that Theo had attended. Obe had determined in his heart to pay for school, board, and lodging. After he had spent a few days with Theo and his family, he found a job as a bus boy very close to the university. After school he worked late into the night at the diner. In a way this was good for him because he was sure of a good meal at least once a day. He was a young man who gave his very best both at school and work. He was loved by those he worked with. I am sure they could not understand how he could be so full of fun even though he had very little sleep and rest. I am convinced it was the Lord who was always by his side. He made many friends very easily.

Apart from working in the diner, he took care of people's gardens on Saturdays. He had a terrific voice and loved to sing. He had a way not only with children but adults too. Although earning an income and doing a good job at school was hard, he always made time to enjoy the people around him. He made the best of every minute God gave him. He never told us about the difficult times he went through. We only heard of it when we moved to the USA ourselves.

At the seminary, he met his wife-to-be. Her name was Raquel. Obe continued to work and study diligently. He had finished both his master's and had proved to be a fantastic preacher. He loved preaching, but his heart was with the children. He wanted to work with children.

Raquel and he got married. Both of them were hired by the International Christian School. Raquel became a teacher and Obediah became the principal of the same school. He loved it. He also got to be the associate pastor of the First Baptist Church, which founded the International Christian School. Although he was not a paid staff member of the church, he gave his best for both the school and church and used his beautiful voice to sing in the church. He was loved by the children, parents, and parishioners. His office at the school was always open for any student who needed to speak with him. I remember seeing not only the older kids walking in but the young kindergarteners too. They were not scared of the principal. They felt he was someone they could talk to without being afraid. Hence, there were very few discipline problems. Parents too were very comfortable to discuss any concerns they had. They knew Obe would listen and if possible, give them help or advice.

GOD'S PLAN FOR PATRICIA AND KUMILA

Meanwhile, Kumila finished school. She was eager to move to London and take up nursing. God answered her prayers, and the door opened for her to go to London. This was an idea which was inconceivable. For a young, single Indian girl to cross the ocean and move to another country was unusual. But nothing in God's plan is unthinkable. And so, after all the paperwork was completed, we said good-bye once again to another family member.

I can't imagine what went through my mother's mind. All I can say is, be careful what you ask of the Lord and accept it when it comes to fruition. My parents had asked the Lord to open doors and give opportunities to their children and He in His own time created the opportunities for them. Who was she to stand in the way? Believe me, it wasn't easy for my mom to let one of her daughters go, but she did. When we trust the Lord with our life and that of our family, we need to be ready to say yes to Him, even when it could break our hearts. God always knows what is best for us and we have no right to stand in the way if we desire to see Him complete the task He has already started.

Life was not easy for Kumie, but she knew that she had to do her best. She wasn't afraid of hard work if it helped her to achieve her goal. And so, she worked two shifts so as to finish her training, as well as provide for herself. I am sure she sometimes deprived herself of eating and sleeping so that she could not only complete her training but be the best at her job and attain the ultimate goal in her life. And with God's help, she did. Within a few years, she was in a very responsible position where she supervised many who worked under her. This happened because my parents had prayed and trusted God for the future of their children and He had answered their prayers. Kumila made the best of the opportunity given to her and was successful.

Patricia continued to excel at work and took on more responsibilities. She began to attend the Lower Circular Baptist Church, which was very close to home. She made many friends and was very popular. She met Keith Pathe who was a prominent member of the church. He had graduated from a renowned Christian school that catered to the children of parents who held high positions. He seemed to love the Lord and came highly recommended. Soon a friendship developed between him and Patricia. Keith's uncle who was his sole guardian was also very fond of Patricia. On the recommendations of many parishioners at the church she attended, Patricia finally decided to get married. Mom gave her a fantastic wedding. Fortunately, they lived a few blocks away from us, and Rajini and I often spent time with Patricia and she with us. They seemed to have a wonderful marriage and we were happy for them.

But a day came when Patricia and Keith decided to move to Australia. We really thought that would be sometime in the future, but things seemed to move so fast that before we knew it, it was time for them to depart. Another member of our family was about to leave. I wondered how Mom would handle it again. She did not say a word. Instead, she helped Patricia with all that was needed to be done for a safe departure. I am sure she shed many tears when we were not watching, but we saw none of that. We went once more to the airport to say goodbye to Patricia and Keith who were immigrating to Australia. Can you visualize the picture? My mom, who was from a remote village of India, now had children living in America, England, and Australia, two daughters living with her, and a son in India who was well established with a family in Calcutta.

(How did this happen, you ask? It's not fair. Why doesn't it happen to the rest of us who also love God? I think it happened because of two young people who started life with nothing except implicit faith in God, total obedience to Him and hard work with a lot of prayer. I believe God has no favorites but if He has total claim to our lives then He is able to do what he chooses. "Great is His faithfulness".)

Our Lord Must Have Full Control

W hat about me? Were my struggles all over? Now that I had decided to do what I thought God wanted me to do, things should go smoothly. That is what I thought. But it was not what God had planned for me. He did not have full control of my life. Although things looked okay, I was still rebellious. I had to get right with God; He wanted complete surrender of my life to Him and nothing less.

The Almighty God had a plan, one that would bring me to my senses. He knew that from my early childhood days I was very competitive. One day the Youth for Christ Director came to our house and told me that he wanted me to compete in the singing and the preaching contest with the young people. The winner would get a free paid trip including transportation to Secunderabad, a city in Southern India, to compete with competitors from all the states in India. Hundreds of youths would attend the five-day conference. If I won the competition in Calcutta, I would get a vacation paid for by Youth For Christ. That was too good to be true. I took the bait and worked hard to win a free ticket. Believe it or not, I did win the preaching contest and came second in the singing contest and was ready to get away for a few days. Of course, everything else had to wait! I am not sure that my brother Obediah was too excited. He felt there was a possibility that I could change my mind about further education. But he gave in and I left for my vacation as planned.

Little did I realize that God had a special plan for me. He was giving me an opportunity to hear one of the finest speakers, Dr. Sam Komerleson. He did not mince words. He had spent many hours in prayer and he was concerned for the youth of our generation. The competition was finished after the first two days, and I did not do too badly. Now I had no choice but to give my whole attention to the speaker. That day he spoke on how we depend on props which keep us from enjoying the full presence of God. He spoke of Samson, a Benjemite set apart for God. He was never allowed to shave his hair and he was the strongest man in his generation. He took his eyes away from God and got involved with Delilah. He was sure that he would never lose his strength and would still be able to defeat the enemies of God. Delilah, corrupted by the Philistines, found out that Samson's strength lay in his hair. With her help, the Philistines got Samson bound and shaved while he was still asleep. When he awoke, Samson found he was helpless, blind, and imprisoned. He realized that he had forsaken God. He came to his senses. While the Philistines gathered, praising their god for their deliverance from Samson and the Israelites, Samson held onto two of the pillars that supported the roof and pleaded once more of God to avenge himself on the Philistines. He was willing to die with his enemies if only God would give him the strength. He was sure God heard his request and so he pulled on the pillars. The roof caved in, and everyone including Samson was killed. It is said that in his death Samson killed more than he did when he was alive (Judges 16:1-30 paraphrased).

The question Dr. Sam asked in the end was: Who is your prop? Who have you been depending on? "You must die to self and depend on God instead of a prop and you can lead a victorious Christian life." Immediately, I realized that I had looked up to my earthly father. I depended on him. He was my prop. As long as he was alive, I was able to live my life satisfactorily. But the moment my prop was taken away, I had broken down.

At the altar call that night, I submitted to the Lord and made Him the Lord of my life. Of course, it did not mean that from now on my life would be a bed of roses. It would have its ups and downs, and the down time might be worse than the good times. But it did mean that my Lord would always be there for me. He was now my Heavenly Father and unlike my earthly father He would never, ever leave me. If I really belonged to Him and loved and obeyed Him like I should, He would not only lead me but bring me back to my senses, when I strayed, because I was important to Him and I was His child. Nothing would ever separate me from the Lord.

St. Paul in Romans 9:35, *"Who shall separate us from the love of Christ? Shall tribulation, or distress, or persecution or famine, nakedness or peril, or sword?"*

He comes back with a resounding answer in verses 38-39 which says, *"For I am persuaded that neither death, nor life, nor angels, nor principalities, nor powers, nor things present, nor things to come, nor height, nor depth, nor any other creature, shall be able to separate us from the love of God which is in Christ Jesus our Lord."*

I was amazed that Paul could say this with such confidence even though he had been through so much. I vowed to go forward, depending on the Lord to give me strength and guidance. I knew life would not be easy and there were times I felt like giving in, but the Lord continued to be there for me, even during the most difficult times.

Do you have this assurance? You can! Do what I did. Submit to Him, accept His Salvation, and make Him the Lord of your life. He will carry you through life's journey.

I know that my mom was my mentor, even though she did not have the privilege of an education and listening to great Bible teachers like I did. But she was an example of what Christ expects from us if we are redeemed and are true worshipers of our Lord and Savior Jesus Christ. He wants full control of our lives and total obedience at all times.

GOD HONORS *THOSE* WHO HONOR HIM

After I returned from the Youth for Christ Rally in Hyderabad, I was excited to teach full-time and go to college at the same time. Fortunately for me, the Education Department at that time wanted to encourage more young people to become teachers. So, they made a condition for us to accomplish both. In order to work as a teacher, we had to guarantee that we would finish our Bachelor's degree within the four years and get our B.Ed. after that to qualify as a teacher. On the surface, it seemed achievable, but actually doing both was not as easy as it seemed. I left my home by 7:30 in the morning and never returned until ten in the night. I used to be very tired when I came home after evening college. The only thing that looked inviting was my bed. Fortunately, there was about two hours after teaching to correct papers and do my homework before I attended college in the evening.

As I said before, there were many students in the church I attended. Most of us had planned to stay home on Sunday before the week of exams. You see, we did not have units that we could take a few at a time. We had to pass in every subject that was assigned to us for the year if we intended to start the next year of college. As working students, we did not have much time to study. So, staying home to study on Sunday seemed to be the only option we had before the finals that took place at the University.

Pastor Collette, who was very close to the students as well as being our mentor, knew there was a possibility that the students would be staying home on Sundays a few weeks before the finals. He wanted the attendees at the church to know where our priorities should be where God was concerned. So, he decided to speak on topics that would answer this important question in each area of our lives. The last topic was centered on the verse found in 1 Samuel 3:30b where it is written, *"Them that honor me, I will honor."*

A few Sundays before our finals, he decided to speak on worshiping God on Sundays. He said God gave us the fourth Commandment to remind His people to set aside a day every week to meet with fellow believers in church. It was a time to fellowship, hear His word, and sing praises to His name. Sunday was God's time, and unless we were too ill to come, it was expected of us as believers to join the worshipers at church. We must honor Him before we can expect Him to honor what we wanted to do. We had to find time during the week to study for finals. Pastor Collette's message spoke to each one of our hearts, and we vowed to find time every day of the week for study and preparation and not rob God of His time. This was a powerful message, and we took it to heart. We were all there on Sundays and spent extra time during the week to prepare for the exam.

God did Honor us for our obedience to His word. To my surprise, I found I had actually done better than expected and graduated with my BA and B.Ed. before my 22nd birthday. God never requires us to do something without giving us the ability to do it. I was so excited. I had obeyed God, fulfilled my requirements, and was a qualified schoolteacher.

Teaching became part of my life. I loved teaching and I loved the students. By this time, I was teaching the fourth grade. Most of the children in my class were from non-Christian families. They lived very close to our home. My mother encouraged me to let them experience Christmas at our home, so every year I invited my students to celebrate Christmas with us. My class children came over to our home for a Christmas party. Mom went all out to make it special. They had all kinds of goodies, and every child got a little gift to take home.

I did not realize the effect it had on these kids until many years later when I met one of my students in California and one in Canada. Both of these young ladies had married and had children of their own. Their families were now believers and attending church. Both of these young ladies remarked on how sharing Christmas with my family had left a mark on their lives. They told me that it was their first Christmas celebration and that little gift had meant a lot. In fact, one of them had kept hers until she had left Calcutta to move to the USA. They informed me that many of them had started to attend Carey Baptist Church, where some of them had committed their lives to God. God does work in mysterious ways if we are willing to give our all to Him.

One would think that everything was going very well with me at this point. But that was not true. Satan does not give up. He attacks when we think everything is fine. I began to miss Dad and began to question God again. Although I had many people around me that cared, inside I was hurting. I kept up a front because I did not want anyone to know what was really going on inside of me.

As soon as I came home after work, I would close the kitchen door, go to the back balcony, and weep my heart out. In India, we did not speak to psychologists. We tried to keep it to ourselves and pretend everything was fine. Fortunately, I knew a Christian couple in Australia with whom I communicated through mail. They understood my pain and sent me a book entitled, From Prison to Praise. They told me that Satan would love to imprison me in my sorrows. The only way to get out was to recognize God's goodness. They advised me not to give in to Satan. Instead, whenever I felt down, I was to find something I could thank God for.

The next day when I was ready to feel sorry for myself, I went to my private place and shut the door after me. Then I just thanked God for the little things I had enjoyed during the day. Immediately I felt different. It was as if my load became lighter. I loved singing and began to sing, "What a friend I have in Jesus, all my sins and griefs to bear." That did it. It was like Jesus had come alongside and carried the heavy load for me. I continued to do this whenever I felt lonely. Within a few weeks, "Praise God," I was healed. God had defeated Satan in my life and I knew for sure that with God by my side, Satan's endeavor was a lost cause. I was whole again, and I could "lean on the everlasting arms."

I wonder if you have a burden you feel is weighing you down. Satan wants you to feel there is no hope. Please do not believe him. He is a liar and he wants to destroy you. Do what I did. Take it to the Lord in prayer. Start counting the blessings God has bestowed on you and praise Him for it. Believe me, if you continue to praise Him throughout the day, Satan will flee from you because He will realize your faith is grounded on the solid rock, the rock Christ Jesus. Please do not let Satan destroy you!

You are a child of God and He loves you and will always be there for you. 1 Peter 5:7, *"Casting all your cares upon him for he cares for you."*

GOD TURNS PAIN INTO JOY

Back in Australia, Patricia and Keith had arrived, ready to begin a new life. They found a house and my sister hoped for not just a new beginning but a great one. Patricia, with all her experience, found a good job quickly and worked hard to make the best of her new life. Within a few weeks she had proved to be not only a good worker, but a very pleasant person to work with. I think her colleagues must have been amazed by her contagious laughter, beautiful personality and the energy with which she did her work. Slowly but surely, she not only became popular but was given more responsibilities which she took in her stride and allowed her to bring more money home.

But although things moved forward at work, life at home was changing. She took the housework seriously. She cleaned and cooked delicious food, always having hot meals ready for her husband at all mealtimes. But no matter how hard she worked at home or at work, she was never able to please Keith. He expected more. Since he always had servants in India to take care of his needs, he felt it was his right to expect Patricia to do the same in Australia. So instead of appreciating her hard work, he considered it was her duty to cater to all his needs. He felt he had a right to live the luxurious life he was used to in India. Instead of treating Patricia as a wife, he treated her as a servant who had to be available at his beck and call. She had to be the breadwinner and also a servant to answer his beck and call.

I can't imagine what I would have done in her place. I am amazed that Patricia agreed to do what was demanded of her. Instead of complaining, she took on two shifts to pay for her mortgage whilst Keith found other things to occupy his time. He became abusive, both physically and emotionally, but Patricia continued to accept it because she felt that marriage was for better or for worse. Besides this marriage vow, two of her brothers were ministers in America and she felt she could not bring shame on their ministry. Perhaps she was also reminded of Mom and Dad and their example of a marriage founded on biblical principles. All this was a heavy weight on her, but she was determined to stick to it with the help of God.

What was amazing was that even though we were a close-knit family, she felt ashamed to share it with us. I wonder, does God really expect His children to die of abuse rather than to be separated from an abusive husband? I don't think so. I believe that we as believers have become so legalistic about our interpretation of God's written word that we assume we have the right to look down and shun those who are forced to seek a way out. In our "holier than thou" attitude, we think we have the right to judge instead of praying for the situation we become critical of it. I think the role of a believer is to come to the aid of the abused. That person needs a friend, someone who is able to direct her/ him to a pastor or a Christian counsellor who is able to help the abused to feel safe. Besides, Jesus reminds us in Matthew 7:1-2, "For with the judgement with which ye judge, ye shall be judged and with the measure with which ye measure, ye shall be measured again."

As I am writing this, I begin to understand that as Christians we are sometimes a hindrance to a solution instead of being a problem solver. I think with our lofty expectations we forget that we are humans and to err is human. If I expect God to forgive me then I should be willing to give a listening ear to one who is going through deep waters instead of sitting in judgement and driving the suffering one to a place of no return.

Three good things happened next for Patricia. Rajini, the youngest in the family, took time off work and visited Patricia in Australia. She thereby gained firsthand knowledge of what was going on. She gave comfort, helped with the cooking, and gave Patricia moral support. She returned to the US and subsequently updated us with what was happening in Patricia's life.

It brought tears to our eyes when we fully understood what had been happening all those years when Patricia had pretended everything was fine. But the situation for Patricia seemed to changed.

The religious Sisters of Charity at St Vincent's Hospital where Patricia worked came to her aid. They offered her accommodation within the hospital complex. Theophilus, the eldest brother, sent a letter assuring her of his support in her course of action. As a result, Patricia left her house with the bare minimum of possessions and found solace in her new lodgings.

Some people say, "God is dead. He is not interested in our day-to-day activities." This cannot be true. Granted, Patricia went through a most difficult period in her life, but God had not abandoned her.

He had a plan for her escape. She ended up living among people who cared. She no longer feared for her life. God had seen her tears and He had intervened. He had given her hope, happiness, and security.

Before ending this chapter, I have a question for you, the reader, and myself: Are we part of the problem or part of the solution? This world would be a better place if we concentrated on being a part of the solution. Let us not be part of a group that finds pleasure in gossiping about others. For we become part of the problem. None of us are perfect. We would want someone to have empathy when we are in pain. With the help of God, may we always be there to comfort, encourage, and uplift others. This will help not only in setting the direction for a new beginning but bring resolution instead of adding to the problem.

TRAINED TO SERVE

In London, Kumila seemed to make big strides with all the hard work she had put in. She had grown up to be very confident in what she did and how she carried herself. She was now a British citizen who was able to make frequent visits to Europe and a few visits to India. On one of her visits, she told mother of the young Indian man she had met in England whom she planned to marry. His name was Biswanath Giridhari Jadunath. She seemed to be very excited. Now that she had told Mother about it, she was ready to tie the knot.

I am sure she would have liked to have a grand wedding with all her family present. But this was not possible. With the help of the church and some of her friends, it turned out to be a beautiful wedding and it was surely blessed by God. We were so glad that Theo was able to make the trip to London to attend that auspicious occasion. It was very special for Kumila who made a beautiful bride. I am sure Theophilus was proud to walk her down the aisle and give her away. Even though the reception was small, the occasion was great and a day Kumila and Bis would remember for the rest of their lives. They made a fine couple who were loved by their friends and members of the church.

I am sure having the moral support of her husband enabled Kumila to be more zealous in establishing the new home they were able to purchase. It was situated in a very convenient spot with public transportation close to the house. By this time, she had made very good Indian friends who were closer to her than her sisters back home in India. They were always there for her.

I think Mom was elated every time Kumila visited India. We had a wonderful time together, but because of the distance and the fear of getting sick, further trips were not possible. I am glad that having families there who cared for her was very special for Kumie who had left home while still young. It is always good to have someone close to share both the joys and sorrows of life.

A few days after her wedding, we were faced with an unforeseen situation. Theophilus, who was driving a beautiful car, was hit by a truck in Fresno, California where he and his family lived. He ended up in very bad shape. The car was completely wrecked, and Theophilus was rushed to the hospital with little hope of survival. He was in a coma with several broken bones and had lost a great deal of blood. There was little chance of him surviving or being normal if he did survive. Doctors were fighting for his life. Again, "what is impossible for man is possible for God." People all over America were praying for him as were the doctors and nurses who were taking care of him. My brother Obediah, who lived in San Francisco, drove several hours a few times a week to be with Sonia and the two girls. Kumila and her husband were trying to find a way to get Kumila to the USA so she could help Theo in the recovery process.

Since we had no phone at home, we did not hear the news. A few days after the incident, Obediah called Zechariah who had the phone. It was the most difficult time for Mother because we had no way of getting the news. She had to wait for Rajini and me to somehow connect with Zechariah to get the latest news. All we could do was pray and weep.

(But we have a God who is omnipresent and all knowing. He had heard the prayers of all the people in America and across the world, including the loved ones in Calcutta and in His time would perform a miracle. You may ask, "Why would a loving God allow such a horrible thing to happen?" He always has a reason and He always knows what is best for His children. We with our human minds cannot comprehend it and get anxious and upset. God sees the greater picture and it is to glorify Himself. As humans, we must leave it in His hands, obey what He tells us to do, and trust Him to do the rest. He never forsakes His children especially in times of despair.)

I think Kumila and her husband had a very difficult decision to make. She was the only one in the family who could assist Theophilus during his recovery. She had the experience of working with patients after a severe accident and my brother would need it when he came home from the hospital. Somehow, we had faith he would recover and after several days in a coma and a great deal of transfusion of blood, Theo finally showed signs of recovery. Though very weak, he was alert.

He was in no position to walk on his own. The doctors and nurses gave their best, and the Lord had done the rest.

After many days of further treatment, he was allowed to go home for rest and undergo further therapy. Kumila took leave from her work and was there, not only to assist Sonia and the children but to help Theophilus fully recover from the results of a severe accident. She was determined to make Theo take his first steps on his own. She did not want him to depend on a walker or a cane for she knew from experience that once a patient depended on a walker or cane, he would never have confidence to walk unaided. So, with much care, encouragement, and determination, Theo began taking a few steps with Kumila by his side. This helped in the healing process and gave him the confidence he needed to continue on his own. He made great progress and was almost back to normal.

Kumila was able to leave Theo and his family and go back to her husband and her job. I am sure she felt relieved after a job well done. It was a great sacrifice on the part of the newlyweds, but I am sure they felt rewarded when they saw the result. This is what God expected of them, and they had passed the test. God expects the same of us as members of the family of God.

We all have God given gifts and abilities. Since it is a gift from God, we need to keep an eye on those of our family who might be in want of encouragement, help, or going through a difficult time financially or physically. As members of the family, we must be available to step in, no matter what the cost may be.

Remember, also, no matter what the circumstance may be, if you really love the Lord, He is in control. There is always a reason why He allows His children to go through a difficult situation. We must remember that God has a purpose. Though we love the Lord, we sometimes forget to do what is expected of us, and God, because of His love, wants to remind us that in order for the plan to materialize, we need to do what He says. It took a severe accident to remind Theophilus what he needed to do.

A SILVER LINING BEHIND THE CLOUDS

As I've said before, sometimes it takes pain and suffering to bring us back to what God desires of us. Why would He do such a thing? I think as humans we get so happy and content with everything going very smoothly for us and our immediate family. We are content with what life has to offer us. We feel content to see everything is going as planned and forget to depend on God for what He has next for us. I know because I have been there and had to have a rude awakening.

When Theo realized that God had spared his life, he suddenly became aware of the absence of Mother in his life. He and his wife Sonia were now ready to sponsor Mom to move to America. As soon as he was able, he asked Mother if he could file her papers to come to the USA. In those days, it was easier to sponsor mothers if you had the means to support them. Of course, Mother said she could not leave the girls. She would only come if her girls could come with her. That was difficult because sisters were considered sixth preference on the list. It was not that Mother believed we could not manage on our own, but we were the ones who stayed with her through thick and thin and she would not desert us in favor of a life in the USA.

By that time, both of her daughters were doing well and life was great. When Mom did not hear further from Theophilus, she gave it up as a lost cause.

Although Theo knew that applying for his two sisters to immigrate to the USA with our mother was very difficult, he did not give up. He wanted Mother closer to him, and so in faith he applied for the last three members of his family who were left behind in India. I am sure he prayed for a miracle and God gave him wisdom to complete the application and send it in. (When God is in control, He is able to move every barrier for the one who depends on Him.)

Much to his surprise, the papers went through and the approval for us to emigrate was stamped to be mailed. Theophilus did not waste any time and mailed the documents to us for our approval and signature. It was addressed in my name, and since I was not too eager (because I was afraid of change), I hid the documents among some of my papers and went about my business as if nothing had happened. But God was aware of what was happening in my heart. This was His plan, and He would prove to me that I needed to accept it. I know some of us do not believe in miracles, but I do. I finally gave in and told the Lord that if He really wanted us to move, he had to send three people to me to confirm it. I knew that no one, not even my mother and sister knew about the papers, so I thought that my request to God would not be answered. But nothing is impossible for God and once again He was going to prove it. I know it is wrong to put a condition for God to prove His will, but I think He understood my fear of moving. It was also a great responsibility for me to take care of all the paperwork, our home, and our belongings and start all over again in a new country.

Both Rajini and I had good paying jobs, lots of friends, and a good home. We were independent. But with the move, we would have to start all over again. That was scary. We forgot that God was in charge and He would see us through if we allowed Him to do so.

The next day was Sunday. After church Rose Nawalkar and her husband invited me over for lunch. They worked with students who came to Carey Baptist Church. When lunch was over, they shared what God had told them. They had been praying for me and my family and were convinced that God would open up the doors for us to be with the rest of our family in the USA. I was shocked and told them I had already received papers but was sitting on it because of my fears. They prayed for God to take care of the situation.

The next day I went to work not expecting anything strange to happen. I worked in the Assembly of God's Church School. Two of my closest friends, who were believers, had also been praying for me. During the morning break, one of them came to me and told me that God had revealed to her that very shortly, I would be moving with my family to the USA. Now I was scared. I told her I had the papers but was too scared to move and had hidden the papers from my family. Like a good friend, she said she would pray for God to give me courage.

Later in the day, my other close friend shared what God had revealed to her that there was a possibility that the three of us would emigrate. God had answered my request, and I could not go against His will. After a few days, I told my mother and Rajini that Theophilus had sent the papers but I had hidden them because I was afraid of leaving India and starting all over again. Together we completed the three applications to the best of our ability and sent them in with the required documents proving our identity. We knew that it would take at least a year before anything happened.

But God works in mysterious ways, and our application returned within a few weeks. We had been granted entrance to the USA if we passed the medical exam, had our passports, and fulfilled all the other requirements. We knew this was not possible because those days it took at least a year to get a passport. Besides, the regulation in our school where I worked required me to give my resignation before the end of February in order to get paid for the last three months of work. I could not go without my salary, since I needed the money to make the move. We had an appointment with the special doctors chosen by the consulate. The result was confidential and sealed. It would be revealed after our appointment with the US Consulate, which was scheduled for the end of March. In order to resign with full pay, I had to have my resignation letter on the principal's desk by the end of February. This was a difficult position to be in.

Finally, after a lot of prayer and with much fear and trepidation, I went to speak with Dr. Mark Buntain, founder of the church and school. He was well known as a Bible expositor, a humanitarian, and a man of integrity. Unknown to me, he had observed me as I led the chapel each morning. I told him about my situation. Being a man of integrity, he told me he would not break the condition for a resignation I had signed at my appointment. However, he would try his best to see if he could get an earlier appointment at the consulate. He prayed with me and told me to go back to work because lunch break was over. Later he sent word for me to meet him after work. I did just that. He informed me that as much as he hated to see me go, he would not stand in God's way. He further told me that we had the last appointment with the consulate on the 28th of February.

The consulate was aware that if the family was accepted, he would allow the secretary to type my resignation letter so it would be on the principal's desk that very evening before I went home. That was amazing!

My dad used to say (and I translate), "If God had to send something and had no other way, He would probably break open the roof and send it down."

The dreaded moment for the appointment came. We waited, as the three envelopes with our medical report were opened and read by the consulate. He seemed to have no expression on his face as he read each of the results. It felt as if time stood still. Then he finally got up, extended his hand, and shook each of our hands and said, "Welcome to America." Once again the three envelopes were sealed only to be reopened on our arrival at the Los Angeles airport. We were entitled to travel as an immigrant but would get our Green Card a few days after our arrival in the USA. We could leave as soon as we had all our clearances and our passports in hand as long as it was before the end of June. Then he turned to me and told me, "Young lady, my secretary is available to type your resignation letter, which you need to submit to your principal immediately."

(You see, God can and does intervene and take care of everything in His own way, which is the right way and in His time. There are no shortcuts where He is concerned. We are his children and He is our Lord and Savior. Therefore, we must not only communicate with Him at all times but trust Him to do what is best for us.)

HE IS ABLE TO MOVE MOUNTAINS

Taken just before Sushila & Rajini left India for U.S.A

The three of us (Mom, Rajini, and me) were at this point quite unsure of what was going to happen next. We were of course very excited but unsure as to what was expected of us by God. We still had to go to work but needed to get things rolling if we wanted to leave for America on time. Was God going to do more miracles because humanly it was not possible to achieve what was expected of us? We had to continue to work and of course all the offices closed at five p.m. There was no way Rajini could make it because she had to work till five. We had no transportation of our own, and traffic in Calcutta moved very slowly due to the large number of pedestrians and cars that competed for space on the streets. Although I was able to leave at 3:30 p.m., it was very difficult to make it to my destination on public transport. With the help of the Lord, I was finally able to get my papers in on time and hoped it would be attended to the next day. We had done our best and we knew that God would do the rest.

Meanwhile we had to take care of all the things that we had accumulated over the years. The problem with us human beings is that the moment we are able to purchase things, we begin to collect stuff, which is really not a necessity. As a result, when it was time to move, we found ourselves in a predicament. To decide what is a necessity and what was a luxury became very difficult, but we had to do it. Once we had separated the two groups, Mother took over. She knew of people who needed furniture but could not afford it. She also knew of those who could help us to get rid of stuff. It was amazing to see all the people who stepped forward to help. It was their turn, as they expressed. They had been on the receiving end, and it was now their turn to reciprocate. A neighbor volunteered to get a company to put all the necessities in a crate and ship it to the USA. Of course, we paid for it to be shipped, but the price was very good and we had to do nothing. She organized it and we did not have to worry about it. God is not only interested in the major events in our life but the minute details also.

It seemed that everything on the home front was moving fast. What worried us was that there was no movement with the passports and the other clearances that we needed. We knew that getting all these documents within that short time was next to impossible, but I also knew that it was God who had arranged for us to go to America. He would work out everything even in impossible situations. He wanted us to be patient and depend on Him. So that gave me an idea. Every day after school, I went to the passport office, signed in, and read my book or corrected my papers as I waited patiently for my turn. Last day of school was the 31st of May. So now I had all day to wait. I did so for a few days. I think the workers in that office got the message. They were tired of seeing me patiently waiting every day. They took action, and the three passports were suddenly in my hand. The most difficult task was achieved, and we were one step closer to leaving. I had done nothing but wait for the Lord to melt the hearts of those who were in charge.

Things started moving very fast. We had all the documents we needed. Tickets were purchased. Kumila had asked us to make a stop in London on our way to America. The Indian Government allowed us to take only $25.00 each. It seemed a very small amount, but in the hands of the Lord, it was a lot of money. A few days before leaving, I was asked by Mom to meet several people who had a special request for me. They reminded me that our mom was a very special person for them and their families. They had no money with which they could hire transportation to take them to the airport, which was quite a distance away. They wanted to go to the airport to say good-bye to the one who had touched their lives. Would I please make that possible? I was touched; however, I knew this was very difficult, because we would need a bus to transport all those people.

The Assembly of God's Church School was the only one I knew had a big bus. I thought I would offer to pay for the loan of the bus and driver, but the driver volunteered his services free of charge and the principal offered to let me have the bus at no cost. I think that was of God. For most of the people this was their first time travelling in style and the first time they had seen an airport and they were very excited and grateful. What a sendoff for one who had come from a remote village in India! Indeed, we are children of a King and He always has the best plan for His children.

We finally said our good-byes and the airplane took off. The flight was long and tiring. We had a stopover in Copenhagen before we got to London, when we discovered we had no hotel reservation and we could not stay at the airport for the night. So, we had no other choice but to use the $75 for a hotel and transportation. Now we did not have any money and we were on our way to a new country. The next morning, we left the hotel without dinner the previous night and no breakfast. But that did not dampen our spirits. We were on the way to the "Promised Land." We were very tired when we arrived at Heathrow airport, but seeing Kumie and Bis gave us the confidence that all was well. We spent a few wonderful days in London and left for America with courage and excitement and with some money in our pockets. Though the journey was long, we waited in great anticipation to meet our two brothers, their wives, and Theo's two children.

The plane was a few hours late when it arrived at LA Airport. Then we had to go through the immigration process, which seemed endless. Finally, we met Theo and his family. It was past midnight before we got into the car and drove to Fresno, which was a few hundred miles from the airport. We had our first experience of the famous "Tule Fog," where it was not possible to see the car in front or on the side of the car. We were scared and tired but ecstatic when we finally arrived home. It was a journey to remember, a journey where we had seen the hand of God at work.

A NEW BEGINNING

Although Theo and Sonia's home was very beautiful and comfortable, it felt a bit strange. Except for Theo, no one understood Mom. This was the first time we were not independent. Theo and Sonia were very kind and generous and their children were cute, but it did not feel like home.

A few days later, Obediah and his wife Raquel showed up in Fresno. It was another great reunion, especially for my mom. She had missed her youngest son, and now she was going to be close to both the eldest and youngest. We had a great time with the two brothers, their wives, and the two grandchildren. But soon things would change. The brothers decided that Mother and Rajini should live with Theo and Sonia and I had to live in Daly City with Obediah and Raquel, which was at least three and a half hours away from Fresno. How could this happen? It was difficult to begin life in this new country and painful to be separated for the first time in our lives. I think that even though Obediah and Raquel tried to make the journey back to their home interesting and comfortable, I was not in a very happy mood. I think I was scared. Since I was an introvert, living apart from Mom and Rajini would make it very difficult for me to share my joys and sorrows. Now don't get me wrong. I think my brother and his wife were beautiful people who probably did not understand how I felt being separated from Mother and Rajini. They were loved by all at the church they attended and the school they worked in. They were very popular. They sure tried to make life comfortable for me. The problem was me. I found it difficult to communicate and adjust to this new life.

In Obediah and Raquel's beautiful home, I had my own room for the first time in my life.

However, I had no experience working with a gas stove and the washer and dryer that made laundry so easy. I did my best to help out, but it seemed that everything was so different in America and even the simplest job seemed scary. This fear prevented me from enjoying the new life that God had made available to me. Having to depend on someone else for my board, lodging, and transportation was a very difficult "pill to swallow."

I hoped I could find a job and earn my own living and get back to the three of us living together. Unfortunately, some people I met convinced me that my teacher's training and experience in India would not be acceptable in California. That was when I began to doubt God's calling for me to be a teacher. I was so filled with despair, that I began to wonder why I had trusted Him and moved to the USA. I had no job, no money, no home, and no friends. I didn't even have my sister and mom to talk to. I could not even return to India because I had nothing to return to. I knew God had not forsaken me but I continued to feel sorry for myself and wondered if I had made the wrong choice.

Meanwhile, Rajini had found a job in Fresno, but it was not close by. Although she had to walk a few blocks to the bus stop to get to work, she was happy. She felt she was not a burden to anyone, and having money in her pocket and being able to pay for her board made her feel independent. Mom too was happy; she was able to keep busy when she was alone at home. She enjoyed taking care of the beautiful flowers, the vegetable garden, the chickens, and the turkey. Theo and Sonia also had a dog, which got thoroughly spoiled by our mother. All this kept her busy during the day when she was by herself.

Though she could not communicate with her grandchildren, she was always eager to see them when they returned home from school. Monica, who was older, always found something to occupy herself with after school, but Christina, the younger one, was very close to her grandmother and spent a lot of time with her. Tina did not know Oriya, yet they got on well. They spent a lot of time together which was very good for Mom and they really seem to have a fun time doing so. This was very strange. Neither understood the other's language and yet they had fun. We might call it "the language of love." Although Tina was very young, she was determined to teach her grandmother a few English words as they tried to communicate. I think this broke down a lot of barriers in Mom's life. Rajini would give her mom a few dollars. She would save the money to take her grandchildren to the skating rink and buy them snacks.

Mother and Rajini began to adjust to this new environment. It was strange to see how well Mother communicated with everyone. Though our mother was alone all day, she made the best of her situation and enjoyed her grandchildren, but her greatest joy was to see Rajini come home after a hard day's work. She was proud of her and couldn't wait to talk to someone she not only loved but could share the happenings of the day with. She could communicate and be her normal self. For her it was difficult to live in this new country, but she was determined to make the best of the situation she was in.

My sister loved music and she bought herself a radio, and the music uplifted her spirit. When she came home from work, she and Mother would spend time together. I know they missed me, especially when they were unable to communicate with me. They looked forward to the time when we would be able to live together even if it meant we had to get a small apartment.

GOD HAS A PLAN FOR ME

eanwhile, nothing had changed for me. Although it was only a few weeks since I had come to live at Obediah and Raquel's house, the days seemed endless because I spent most of my waking hours by myself. Both Obediah and Raquel left for work by 7:30 a.m. and did not return until after six. Even though I helped to clean and cook, time seemed to stand still for me. Unfortunately, I did not know how to cook American food and was too nervous to use the stove or oven. I only cooked Indian food, which I think Obediah enjoyed as it reminded him of Mother's cooking. Raquel was not used to Indian food but did not complain. She tried to eat whatever was cooked.

How I longed to be independent and get back to teaching. I missed getting up in the morning, to get ready for school, and be with those beautiful children and my co-workers. There was never a dull day with correcting papers, preparing for the next day, and working in the garden. Now I had no one to communicate with and no garden to maintain or the beautiful flowers to enjoy. My future seemed bleak.

On Wednesdays one of my brother's friends took me to an evening Bible Study and Prayer meeting at the Church. Although I was reluctant to participate, I did enjoy going every week. There was an elderly gentleman in the church who was a podiatrist and had five grown up girls. He addressed me as "Smiley" and said I was his sixth daughter. I think that was very special. He always made me feel welcome at church. Since both my brother and sister-in-law worked in the school, they met me at church and brought me back home after Bible Study.

One day Obediah came home from work very worried. He could not find a substitute teacher for one of his staff members who had taken a few days off. In desperation, he asked if I would be willing to take her place for a week. I was afraid but willing to give it a try. I actually enjoyed it and felt more confident than I did before. I was also glad to be employed even though it was for a very short time.

Later in the week, Obediah took me to a Christian bookstore near the church and school. They needed an extra worker at the store. It was an opportunity for me to work in a Christian bookstore if I was willing to give it a try. I went for an interview and was accepted. The pay was very small and it was in the city, but I would be employed. I could easily get there on public transport. I accepted and started working a few days later. Since the bookstore was open six days a week, I was asked to work from Tuesday to Saturday every week. I was off Sunday and Monday. My boss was a God- fearing man who was very compassionate and took time to help me adjust. I was a fast learner and felt good that I finally had a job.

It was a wonderful experience. People seemed to come into the store to meet the "strange Hindu woman" as they addressed me, since I was dressed in Indian clothes. They felt they had to talk to me and wondered what a Hindu woman was doing in a Christian bookstore. (Most people in America did not know that not all Indians were Hindus.) Others were surprised at my British accent. You would probably consider them rude, but I think it was God's way of getting me out of my "shell." I was forced to communicate, which helped me to talk about myself and give my testimony. They congratulated me for speaking English fluently and were surprised to note that I had been an English teacher in India.

God is amazing. He knew how to deal with every situation in our lives. He never makes a mistake. He had brought us to America and He had something special in store for each one of us. This was His way of getting me ready for the job He had in mind. I was so excited when I got my first paycheck, which was very small and I needed a lot of things. The next day was Sunday and I was immediately reminded of tithing.

(I needed the money to buy a few essentials, but God reminded me of the message Pastor Colette had preached on when He explained Malachi 3:10 and I quote, "Bring ye all the tithes into the storehouse, that there may be meat in mine house and prove me now herewith, saith the Lord of hosts, if I will not open you the windows of heaven, and pour you out a blessing, that there shall not be room enough to receive it."*)*

That was enough to restore my dependency on the Lord God Almighty. In order to see Him prove Himself to me, I had to obey His request, and I did. I made the right choice. God never lies. He always does what he says in His own time. He did open the "windows of heaven and poured out His blessings" which I am still enjoying. I determined in my heart that day that no matter what life throws at me, I will never look back but look up to the giver of all gifts.

I continued to work at the bookstore, but this time not because I had to but because I chose to. It was amazing how my attitude had changed. I looked forward to going to work and I began to enjoy it. Everything seemed to change even though it was the same job. I believed that this job was of the Lord and I was going to enjoy it.

GOD WORKS IN A MYSTERIOUS WAY

At about this time Patricia, my eldest sister, decided to visit us in America. That was great. She had a way of bringing joy and laughter wherever she was and she made me smile again. It was Monday, and normally I stayed home for my day off. But that Monday I was at work. On Saturday my co- worker had been very sick, so I volunteered to give her my Monday, so she could have a long weekend to recuperate. Obe and Raquel were also at work, so Pat had to take the telephone calls which was good. Pastor Higgs thought I was at home and called to let me know that there was a need for an Assistant Director in a Christian day care center and he had set up an appointment for me to go for an interview. Had I been at home, I would have refused to go. God knew that beforehand and He had Patricia answer the call. She had more confidence in me than I had in myself. She said I would be there because I would be home on Tuesday.

She was so excited that she could not wait to tell me the good news. Of course, I was not as excited as she was. Immediately, I said I was not going, but Patricia had made up her mind, and as the younger sister, I was expected to take her advice. She convinced me that I was qualified and able to take the position. I doubted that but did keep the appointment. The director was a beautiful young lady, the wife of a pastor. We got on well, and I felt comfortable. She read my recommendations, saw my certificates, asked me a lot of questions, and immediately hired me. My salary was almost double of what I was getting at the bookstore and the school was closer to Obadiah's house. Of course, I had to get the necessary units required for being an assistant director of a day care center. She convinced me I could do that at the evening classes offered at the state university. One of the ladies of their church even volunteered to give me a ride to and from the college. It seemed everything was planned for me in advance so I accepted the job.

I gave my two week's notice at the bookstore and began the new job on the first week of February. Things moved so fast that I had no time to worry. It was strange that I did not have to look for a job; the job came looking for me! God is faithful. He does His part if we are willing to do what He asks of us and that is to place implicit trust in Him.

As an assistant director, I got to work in the office, meet parents, work with teachers and with the children at least for two hours a day. Being with the kids was the best part of my day. The children were between the ages of 2½ to 5 years. Although it was a day care center, we did include a lot of teaching too. I believed that children in their early childhood years should be exposed to the gospel. So I introduced a morning worship time. They loved music and story-time and I loved teaching them. So, every morning before we served them snacks, we had a special time for singing and a Bible story. It was amazing how the children responded. Though I was supposed to work for eight hours a day, I was there from the time it opened until the time it closed. I really enjoyed it!

Unexpected Promotion

Three months later, the director and one of the board members met with me for a special discussion. Unknown to me, the director was pregnant and wanted to retire after two more months of work. She had to get an understudy to make sure everything ran smoothly after she left. She said she had observed me and would like to offer the job to me. Rosalie (a board member) would be in the office to help me with the paperwork and bookkeeping, and I would be in charge of directing the school. She felt that I was the best choice. Rosalie also told me that as a director my salary would double. This was tempting but also a great responsibility. I think I was afraid, but both of them assured me I was capable and they would be there to train me before I took full control. Their confidence in me and also their support I felt that with God's help I could do it. So I finally accepted the position. Fortunately for me, by that time I would also have the units required by the state to hold that position.

I was amazed with the way the Lord had worked out the minute details for me. To think I had spent so much time feeling sorry for myself, when all long the good Lord knew what He had planned for me and His plan is always for the best. He had not forgotten me. He was with me and had to prepare me for the position He had planned for me. His ways were definitely far superior to my way, and I am glad I had obeyed Him.

I was very excited and wished I could share the news with Rajini and Mother but waited until the time was right. When Rajni heard the news, she decided to move to Daly City and find a job. She was successful in finding a job in the city of San Francisco. We hoped that now we had two paychecks, we could afford a small apartment. After searching high and low, we finally found a two-bedroom, two-bathroom apartment in Daly City just near the public transport. Both of us had saved enough money to buy the bare essentials and pay the advance rent.

Moving into an apartment was very exciting even though we knew that living on our own would be financially difficult. I think Mother was excited the most. Living with Theo and Sonia had been great. She had everything she needed, but being back with the girls was what she wanted. She was ready to join us even when we told her it would be awhile before we could have everything we needed.

I know some people might think it strange for two young women to live with their mother, but to us it was one of the greatest blessings in life. Our mother wanted to be there to support us and take care of our home, so we could do what was needed to begin this new life. Most of all she wanted to be with us, to encourage us and help us out. She knew how to make a little money go a long way. We were really fortunate to have a mother who cared. Once again, the Lord had brought the three of us together and we were confident that with His help and the joint efforts of the three of us, we could accomplish great things. Being a director was great, but it was a position with great responsibilities. I was not only accountable to the board members, the staff, the children, and the parents but also to the Social Services Dept. who seemed to doubt the ability of someone from a third world country. This could have been a negative experience for me. Instead it forced me to do my best, and it became a great learning experience. Rosalie volunteered to be the bookkeeper which gave me all the time needed to help the children, support the teachers and workers, and encourage the parents. Taking care of these three areas are essential for the education of the children. Developing a good Christian educational environment for the child helps parents understand the value of a Christian education, which is vital for a child's growth. This is what the Lord would have me do, and I aimed to achieve it. Although it was difficult and tiring, the day care center began to flourish.

Later, when I floated the idea of making the day care into a pre-school, I received 100% support from all concerned. Within a few months, we found extra space, a qualified kindergarten teacher, and children to attend the new Rainbow School. The parents helped me build a new playground with play equipment for the children. The enrollment had increased from less than 50 to 80 children of which some were part time pre-schoolers. What was even better, the finances went from a negative to positive territory. I was no longer a timid person who was scared to venture out, but had become confident enough to move on and see what the Lord had in store for me.

PATRICIA AND STUART

Patricia and Stuart Wedding

Back in Australia, things were beginning to change for the better for Patricia. After many, many weeks, she received the news that her estranged husband Keith had died. He had been dead for a few days before word got out. This was sad but a relief for Patricia knowing that she would no longer live in fear of seeing him suddenly appear at work or other places. She finally felt free to live her life.

In time she met Stuart Huish, who seemed so different to Keith. She had found a good friend who shared in her laughter and her tears. He seemed to be well liked by everyone at the office. Having observed him at work and seeing how he interacted with other employees made her feel that here was a gentleman who respected others even though they had to work for him. He seemed to treat both the male and female employees with a firm but gentle approach. This made her comfortable to be with him, and they soon realized that it would be good for them to get engaged and begin life together. Of course, they had to do the proper thing and that was to call our mother and ask if that was acceptable. Can you imagine our surprise when we got a call from Australia and both Stuart and Patricia were on the other end? We had heard of Stuart and he seemed to be a good man, but remembering all that Patricia had been through during her first marriage did make us feel wary. We were sure glad she had waited a while at least until Keith had passed away before deciding to take this step.

We waited patiently to hear what Mother would say now that Stuart had asked for her blessing. She had never met Stuart, and we thought she would immediately advise Pat to think hard and wait a while before making a decision. I think I was surprised when she asked us to tell Stuart and Patricia it was okay with her. I knew our mother always prayed for each of her children and asked God to not only protect us but guide us in the right way. I think she understood what life had been for Patricia and all she had been through in a strange country and all alone. She had spent hours praying for her and she would trust God to take care of Patricia as she took this new step. She deserved to be happy. She would pray for both Stuart and Patricia as they considered this new life together.

I think both Patricia and Stuart were surprised that Mother had given her consent and started making plans for this new phase of their lives. We couldn't be there for them, but they seemed to have friends both at work and church that would do everything to make this occasion a day to remember. We continued to pray for them. Mother longed for Patricia to have a wonderful experience that would erase whatever she had been through before. Although she could not be there physically, she was there in the spirit and asked God to bless the couple. The tedious wait was over and they were ready to begin their new life together. They were married with their friends and co-workers as witnesses. We couldn't wait for the pictures to arrive. Pat sure made a beautiful bride.

Initially Pat and Stuart lived close to the city but eventually bought a beautiful place in the country, the kind Patricia really enjoyed. For the first time, she had a huge open place to keep ducks and chickens, and had a beautiful flower and vegetable garden. It was hard work but it brought her great joy. Life was good. She still enjoyed her work and the people she worked with, but after a while I think Patricia was ready to take early retirement while her husband Stuart continued to work. She sure deserved to take life easy after what she had been through. God had given her a second chance and what a blessing it was.

Although she did not have to go to work, she had lots to do in this beautiful place away from the city and all its noises. She loved caring for their birds in the aviary, the chicken, the ducks, collecting fresh eggs every morning, tending to the vegetables and the flower gardens. The best part was that they were visited by many exotic Australian birds. Imagine eating your breakfast as you watched and fed those exotic birds in the backyard! It was a sight for sore eyes. I know it was the best part of my day when we visited them in Australia a few months later.

What a reunion! Kumila, Bis, Mum, Rajini, and myself travelled to Australia to see them. Accommodating us was a challenge but being out in the open was worth it all. I loved the outdoors and spent as much time there as possible. We also visited a few surrounding places. We had a great time together, but the days flew by. We had to go back to work. Saying goodbye to the couple was very difficult. As a family, we were very happy for Patricia and Stuart and prayed God would grant them many more wonderful years in which to share their beautiful life together.

GOD'S PROVISION

Back at home things were beginning to settle down. Rajini was still working in the city and commuting by bus and BART every day. She had a car and was a very good driver, but trying to commute during office hours was tedious and time consuming. Parking in the city of San Francisco was not only very expensive but the parking lot was far from the place of work. Taking all this into consideration, it was advisable to take the bus and the BART (Bay Area Rapid Transit) back and forth from work. The only problem was that she had to leave the house before 5:10 in the morning and return after 5:30 p.m.

By this time, I had learned to drive and was able to buy a used Toyota Corolla car. What a difference it made to my commute and confidence! I saved over an hour going back and forth from school. Fortunately, I did not have to drive to the city, which would have been very challenging.

Rajini loved driving her car, which was large and quite comfortable, during the weekends. Mother was very observant, and even though she didn't drive, she could actually direct someone to the places we drove to. Now that we had a reliable car, it gave us great joy to go crabbing on Saturday mornings. Rajini loved fishing on the pier, and when she saw the people crabbing, she began to join them. Even though we caught very few, we came home with almost a bucket full of crabs. You see, the men who caught crabs broke their legs off and instead of throwing them back into the ocean they gave us the body which we found delicious when it was cooked Indian style. Can you imagine eating crabs at least four or five times a month? I don't think we could complain about that. Not only did we enjoy the crabs but also saved a great deal of money. Fortunately, the Bay those days was very clean and it was safe to eat the crabs. Besides, fresh crab from the Bay tasted really good! We had to admit that God did provide for His children in mysterious ways...

We discovered that Mother loved walking on the beach as much as we did. So, sometimes on Saturdays Rajini would drive us to a beach a few miles away. Mother enjoyed herself walking up and down the beach while Rajini had something cooking on the grill. It was amazing how spending a day like this thrilled all of us. Occasionally we went away for the weekend to Santa Cruz near the beach. This was Mother's favorite way of spending her birthday, Mother's Day, or any other holiday. She was very relaxed and just enjoyed herself walking on the beach, thrilled when the waves washed over her feet. I don't think we had ever seen Mother so relaxed and so happy. These were precious memories which will always be treasured in our hearts.

I think Rajini and I were the most fortunate among the seven brothers and sisters. We got to see and enjoy our mother when she had no worries regarding the home or her family. For the first time, even though she was in a strange country with people who did not understand her, she was relaxed like a free bird, without a care in the world. Her heart was full of joy because although Rajini and I didn't have a lot of money, we had learned to enjoy a good family time with what we had. We were safe and we had found our niche.

Our mother was content to share her life with us and enjoy it at the same time. She deserved this peace and tranquility after all she went through losing Dad when she was still young and raising six children in a city. We were happy to see how everything turned out so well because of her implicit trust in a God that never fails. It was good to see the desires of my parents fulfilled for their children. She was in a foreign land, with very few friends, but she had her family and she could ask for nothing more.

After working for five years as director of Rainbow School, it seemed fitting to move to a new place of employment. Although I was not too excited about this change, I knew God had a definite plan for me. I was asked by the superintendent and founder of Highlands Christian School to make an appointment with her. I was excited but a bit nervous. The interview seemed to go well. Fortunately for me, one of the teachers at the ECE classes I had attended had seen what I had done at Rainbow School and had given me a high recommendation. Dr. Buntain who was a personal friend of the superintendent had also given a good recommendation. The interview went well, and seeing my qualifications, experience, and recommendations, the Superintendent Mrs. V. Sheley offered the job of first grade teacher to me. Although the Summer School was in session, I was able to start the very next day as a teacher of the prospective kindergarten class. I was amazed to see the salary the superintendent offered. This was of the Lord. I couldn't wait to work as a first grade teacher at the beginning of the new school year.

Meanwhile, Rajini had also moved to a better-paying job in San Francisco. She enjoyed working in the city and used her lunchtime to enjoy the sights and shops close to her office. Sometimes she ate out in a restaurant and made sure we had something to sample from the food she brought home. We as a family were really grateful to God for the way He was providing for all our needs and helping us to make some good memories as we spent time together.

With our combined salary and Mother's encouragement and a lot of prayer, we wondered if we could put a down payment on a little house with a backyard where Mom would have the freedom to have a garden of her own. It would give her something to do and enjoy while we were at work all day. The area where we had our apartment was not very safe and had very little opportunity for Mother to move around.

From The United Kingdom To The United States

J ust about this time, Bis got the opportunity to get a job transfer to Denver, the capital of Colorado. They felt it was a good idea and chose to emigrate to America. They had a few weeks to make this move. Again Theophilus, our eldest brother, sponsored them. Things moved very fast for them. They sold their house and moved to the USA. I think our mother was elated. She could not wait to see them. They stayed with us for a few days. It was fun for the five of us to squeeze into a two-bedroom apartment. Fortunately, we had a living room with a roll-away bed and two bathrooms. It also gave them a short break before they moved to Denver to begin their new life.

They soon moved to Denver, Colorado where Bis began his new job. It was challenging, but he adjusted well and I am sure did a good job. Kumi decided on a new career. She enrolled in college to get her degree in Nuclear Medicine. This was not easy for her. For the first time in her life, she had to learn physics and chemistry. But God had a plan for this difficult situation. Bis, her husband, was very good in both those subjects. Although Kumie had to start from the basics, her husband was able to tutor her and bring her up to the standard she needed to be at. As a result of all the hard work she put in and with the help of the Almighty God, she was able to do well in her finals and graduate from that class. She immediately found a job in a renowned hospital where she enjoyed doing her job with excellence.

They bought a nice big house and began their new life in a new country. They seemed to adjust very quickly and made quite a few friends. I think both of them felt good as they got used to living in Denver. They made a lot of new friends both at work and church, and according to me they had the best garden in and around their area.

Kumila loved working in her garden, which was huge. The beautiful dahlias and roses in her yard were exquisite and envied by all who passed by. They also had a very good vegetable and fruit garden where they grew a variety of vegetables and fruits. Of course, it took a lot of hard work and money, but it was worth it all. What a joy they had when Kumila could go to the garden, pick the fresh vegetables, and produce a delicious dinner for both of them. It was worth all the hard work and time they had put in. I am sure she had longed to do that in London, but due to lack of space she was unable to do much. They were very happy that they had made the move from London to the USA. We were happy too because we could visit and communicate with each other very easily.

MAKING A HOUSE A HOME

After spending many weeks searching for a house, we soon discovered that finding a decent affordable house in and around the city of San Francisco was next to impossible. Since Rajini came home late every evening, the house searching was left in the hands of my realtor and myself. Mother spent a lot of time in prayer and was confident that God would soon find us a house even if it was not spectacular. Just as we were ready to give up, we found a house we could afford though it did not look very presentable. The back and front yard was nothing but hard dirt, rocks, and stones. The inside of the house was less than livable, and the roof had to be taken care of. We were not too excited about it, but Mother felt that with a little hard work this house would become a home for us. We took a step of faith and bought the house. Unfortunately, since we did not have much collateral, our interest rate was very high. Mother was confident that although it would be difficult, we could manage the payments. Even though she did not have an income, she had more faith than we did. So, we took a step of faith and moved in on the night of December 24th, 1985.

Though the house was nothing much, it was ours and we felt proud to have one. All we could say as a family that it was God's doing. Five years before, we had come into this country without a penny in our pockets; five years later we had a second hand car, both of us had jobs, and the three of us had bought a house. This was not our doing; it was God's and He never fails if we allow Him to take control. We committed this home and the three of us into the hands of God.

The next day was Christmas. It was a holiday so we could not get hooked up to electricity and gas and the refrigerator would not be delivered until the 3rd of January. Our new neighbors graciously invited us to share their Christmas family dinner, which was a sight to behold. We had never met our neighbors, but we felt at home in their house. They had accepted us as part of their family and became our closest friends. A new chapter of our lives had begun, and we began the

New Year of 1986 in a house of our own and great expectations from Almighty God and gratitude in our hearts.

If you had seen this house, you would have wondered why we ever bought the place. The renters had completely destroyed everything. There was no carpet, no window curtains, no refrigerator, a broken washing machine, and the house did not look good on both the outside and inside. But this did not bother my mother. Rajini had to go to work the next day. I was on Christmas vacation. So Mother and I just started scrubbing and cleaning the house. What a difference a few days of hard work made in the house. It was actually livable. Rajini's boss offered her not only the choice of the rug she wanted for the house but the workers to put it down. They did a terrific job. The carpets gave a new look to the interior of the house. A new roof was installed by the seller. A few months later, we were able to get curtains for the windows and a washer and dryer to take care of the laundry. Life was not easy, but trusting God had made the impossible a possibility.

A GARDEN TO ADMIRE

Dhalias

Meanwhile, Mother worked hard to remove the rocks from the soil in the front and back garden. Then she put bricks around both the two gardens to make a beautiful border. This was hard work and took a few weeks to accomplish. What a difference her hard work made to both those gardens. She felt right at home and was never afraid of all the hard work. She loved gardening and she was determined to do her part in making the house beautiful for herself and her daughters. So on Saturdays she went with us to get all the flower shrubs and the vegetable seeds of her choice. In a few weeks, she had planted flowers in the front and vegetable plants in the back garden. She even took the time to paint the fence in the front. The white fence looked new and enhanced the look of the "once rejected house." She had promised that with a little hard work the house we had bought would become a home, and it did. We were proud to be the owners of this beautiful house. In her quiet way, our mother had achieved more than we had ever anticipated.

Neighbors stopped by to admire the beautiful flowers in the garden. She was right when she said that with a little bit of sweat and a lot of hard work that same rejected house would become a home. Mother no longer felt lonely. She was busy improving the look of the house and preparing delicious food for her family. She felt good that she was able to not only enjoy her stay in America but also help her daughters establish a home in America. It was always a joy to come home after a hard day's work and smell the delicious Indian food Mother had cooked for us. We had missed eating together since leaving Calcutta, India, and I can honestly say that mother cooked the best meals we have ever eaten.

As I recollect those wonderful days, I get a glimpse of the days before our departure from Calcutta, India. I was scared wondering if we had made the right choice and what would happen to the three of us without money, a home, or a job? I remember studying the book of Joshua chapter 1, where Moses had died and God was calling Joshua to be his replacement. Joshua did not feel qualified to replace a leader like Moses, but God felt otherwise and gave him encouragement and advice. It was a very timely message for me as I thought of our emigration to the USA. Three verses in this particular chapter caught my attention. They were verses 3, 7 and 9b.

> *"Every place that the sole of your feet shall tread upon, that have I given unto you, as I said unto Moses."*
>
> *"Only be thou strong and very courageous, that thou mayest observe to do according to all the law. which my servant Moses commanded thee; turn not from it to the right hand or to the left that thou mightest prosper withersoever thou goest."*
>
> *"Be not afraid. Neither be thou dismayed: for the Lord thy God is with thee whithersoever thou goest."*

God knew of my fears, but He reminded me that we needed to be strong, do exactly what He asked of us, and He would be with us and give us more than what we had hoped for. At that time, I did not give much thought to it because time was short and much had to be accomplished. But now that I look back, I realize that God had given me a promise, and because we stepped out in faith and did what He expected, He had not only fulfilled that promise but went far beyond what we had expected. We had all our needs met and more.

It was amazing to see how the Lord worked the minute details of our lives. Though quite tiring, Rajini continued to work in the city. She worked hard and after a busy day at work and a long bus ride back and forth, she came home thoroughly exhausted. Mom on the other hand waited patiently to see her girls and enjoy a meal together. It all felt good.

Saturday was a special day for the three of us. Rajini set this day aside to help a neighbor who was elderly and unable to do her shopping. She waited for Saturday when Rajini helped her down the steps to do her weekly grocery shopping. It was not an easy task because my sister had to push the wheelchair, but Mother was very happy that her daughter was willing to help a shut-in go shopping at her favorite stores. It was a tedious job for Rajini as she spent almost the whole day wheeling this neighbor to all the stores she wanted to visit. Though it was not easy, it seemed to bring Rajini great joy to be able to help. I must admit that even though she did not mention it, Rajini looked very tired when she returned from her day with Albina.

On the other hand, I spent the day with my mother. Remember, she spent all day during the week by herself. Saturday was her time to get out of the house. We took the public bus everywhere we went. It was always a joy to take my mother to do her grocery shopping. We spent all morning shopping, and even though Mother was very tired waiting for the buses and walking, she never complained. The farmers market was her most favorite place to shop. She loved fresh fruits and vegetables and she enjoyed choosing the ones she knew her daughters loved. After that we went to buy fish and meat. She knew how to pick the freshest fish and the best meat for the best price. I think the best part of my day was to take my mother for lunch. Even though she did not like fast food, she refused to go to a restaurant for lunch. There were two reasons for this. First, she felt it was a waste of hard-earned money, and second, Rajini was not there to enjoy it with us. It did not really matter what we ate; it was the time we spent together that made it so special.

Sunday was an important day. Even though Mother did not know much English, she enjoyed going to church and being a part of the worship service. By this time, she could understand quite a bit of what the pastor preached and had learned to enjoy the hymns and music. Her favorite song was "Amazing Grace." She was glad to be in God's house. The strange thing was that even though she didn't speak the language, she knew God understood her and her desire to worship Him. God is not a respecter of persons. There is no barrier He will not cross if we, His children, choose to love and worship Him.

THE SUN OUTSIDE AND THE SON INSIDE

Obediah and his wife lived very close by. That meant we could visit each other as often as we desired. Obediah took advantage of this as much as he could. Mom always waited in anticipation for his visit. She was comfortable in receiving phone calls because she knew it would be one of her children. She could not wait to hear from Obediah when he called to say he would be visiting, either on his lunch break or after work. Immediately, she cooked him his favorite dish and welcomed him with great joy. Her face just lit up. She had so much to share and it was so easy because Obediah had not forgotten his native language, although he hadn't spoken it for years. He made her laugh and it was like she had never left home in Calcutta. We knew Obediah had visited Mother when we came home from work because we could see the glow on her face and the excitement in her voice as she related to us the time she had spent with her son, our brother.

One day we came home to find Obediah at home and Mother very busy cleaning a large salmon. He had gone deep sea fishing early that morning with his friend Ken. He had caught two big fish. He gave one to his friend and brought the sixteen-pounder home. I know it made our mother very happy to see the fish, but thinking of her son fishing in the ocean made her scared and she made Obediah promise never to do it again. He just laughed and tried to change the topic with all his stories while Mother cleaned, scaled, and cut the fish for Obediah and us. That was the best fish curry we had had since we arrived in America. It is something we will remember for the rest of our lives.

I wish you had met Obediah. I have met many, many people in my life, but Obadiah's personality tops them all. It isn't because he was my brother but someone who was admired by all who met him. It did not matter if he was among little ones or the aged or the ones in between, he was able to make them laugh. It seemed that it was a special gift God had given him. He made friends with everyone, even strangers on our street. His famous words to a passerby at the gate of our house was, "My mom has the sun outside and now she will have a son inside."

One would think he did not have a care in the world. I am here to say he did, but he had the joy of the Lord which he used to attract the ones he met not only to himself but to the Lord he loved and worshiped. I don't think I envy him, but sometimes I wish I could just forget all the disappointments of the world and spontaneously laugh and share the joy of the Lord. He always stopped to talk to our neighbors who lived near us and the ones who were further down the street.

Everyone who met him remarked on how Obediah was like a breath of fresh air. Our mother felt proud of her son as the neighbors expressed their joy at meeting her son Obediah. You see, it is not what you give someone that expresses joy; it is the spontaneous way you react when you meet them. We all leave a mark in this world, but the mark that Obediah left on the people he met will never be forgotten but cherished for a very long time. There is so much sorrow and heartache in this world. He tried to make a difference in the way he was kind and very sensitive to others. There were some who had wronged him and hurt his feelings, but he never held a grudge against them. He continued with life as if nothing had happened. He always knew that God was in control and He would take care of it. His mission was to bring joy and laughter wherever he was and he continued to do so to his very last breath. I have learned a lot from my brother and wish I could tell him so.

Obediah did leave a mark in this world. Little did anyone know that his life would be short-lived. Unfortunately, he developed a heart problem. He was admitted to hospital, but after a few days the doctors released him and gave him permission to fly to the East Coast where he was one of the speakers. Unfortunately, he did not survive to see the next day. He died before the morning came and went to meet his Maker.

We were at work when the Pastor and his wife brought the news to our mother. They tried to comfort her, but because of the language barrier there was very little verbal communication. Imagine our surprise when we came home to find mother weeping her heart out, telling us her son was gone. Pastor and his wife left after I came home. No parent should have to go through what Mother went through that day and the years afterwards. Just when she thought all was well, her youngest son had been taken from her. She didn't even get to say good-bye to him and did not see his body until the day of the funeral, which was almost a week later.

None of us know when we will be called home by the Lord. We cannot take anything with us, but we can leave behind memories. Obediah was only 51 years old, the youngest of the three brothers when he was called home. He will always be remembered by the ones he met and his family who loved and enjoyed him. He had touched our lives in a way that will never be forgotten. Mother had lost a beloved son and we had lost a brother. This was a turning point in our lives especially, for our mother. Nothing anyone could do or say helped to wipe away the pain she experienced.

Although she hurt, she tried her best to hide it from us, but staying alone all day took a toll on her. We lived very close to the graveside. Once in a while, even if she did not ask us to, she was ready with a bunch of flowers to lay on his grave when we volunteered to take her. It gave her some kind of relief, but the pain remained.

Man Looks At The Outward Appearance But God Looks At The Heart

One day I noticed that my face was attracting attention from some passerby. On arriving home, I wondered what had changed and looked at the mirror. For the first time I noticed a white patch on my face. I could not believe it. It was bad enough that I was the shortest in the family with bow legs. I had never been attractive, and somehow, I had become used to it. But now this. People were beginning to stare at me as if I was an alien. I felt uncomfortable going to a beauty salon for a haircut. Rajini, my sister, saw my dilemma and volunteered to give me a haircut although she had never done it before. Believe it or not, she did a fantastic job and it really looked good. I believe that God had something to do with that. Mother convinced me that it would soon disappear, but it didn't. It kept getting worse.

I finally made an appointment with my doctor who sent me to a dermatologist. I soon realized I had vitiligo where my skin was losing pigment rapidly. There was no cure for it except to get it bleached like Michael Jackson, the famous singer, did was what my dermatologist told me. For me this was not a solution. Instead I came home very disappointed. I went on with life as if nothing had happened, but people treated me differently. It was as if I had the plague. Most of them stared and whispered amongst themselves. Some suggested I paint my face. One sales lady even asked me to go to a different line and some refused to serve my mother and me even if I was the next customer.

The worst situation happened on one of our mother and daughter outings on a Saturday afternoon. My mother, who was not feeling too well, wanted to go home, but I convinced her to have lunch before we went home. We found a restaurant close by and signed in. We were asked to wait for our number to be called. We waited patiently outside in the heat of the day and watched as all the customers who came after us were called in to be seated. Finally, Mom suggested we forget lunch and go home. I would have none of it and demanded to be attended to.

I could have called the manager to complain, but my mother did not want a scene. She wanted to go home. So we paid for a lunch we could not enjoy and decided to go home.

I was angry and bitter. I wondered what I had done to cause this to happen. I felt rejected. It seemed my little world had come to an end. It hurt when I felt eyes staring at me. I avoided looking at the mirror in case it frightened me, until one morning God decided to deal with this little problem that was bugging me so much.

The Bible lesson for that day for my first graders was God choosing a king to replace King Saul. I knew this story inside out and was ready to explain it to the first graders who were eager to hear it, but I decided to read it from the Bible first before I shared it with the children. The lesson was taken from the 1st book of Samuel chapter 16 where Samuel the priest was sent to Jesse's house to anoint one of his sons. Jesse had eight sons but the youngest one was in the fields looking after the sheep. Each of the seven was asked to pass before Samuel who had to anoint the one God chose. Samuel was sure that God would choose the eldest one who was tall, strong, and handsome, and would according to the world be the best to serve as a king of Israel. But God did not choose him or the six younger ones that came after him. Samuel could not believe God would make such a big mistake. People would look up to a tall, strong, and handsome king who would demand obedience and respect. But God had not chosen the one Samuel thought appropriate. Instead He wanted the youngest lad who took care of his father's sheep. The Lord in verse 7 rebuked him and said, "Samuel, look not on his countenance, or on the height of his stature; because I refused him; for the Lord seeth not as man seeth; for man looketh on the outward appearance, but the Lord looketh on the heart."

Samuel listened to God. He sent for David and anointed Him who was only a shepherd boy to be the next king. Although he did not look kingly, he was the only one whose heart was totally for the Lord and was ready to take the responsibility of a king seriously. He made mistakes but asked for forgiveness and ended his career pleasing God.

For the first time in my life, the essence of the story became clear to me. There was a big difference between how the world looked at man and how the world sought to give recognition to man. To be accepted by the world, one had to be attractive and sought after. It did not matter what the intention or the heart of man was. On the other hand, God who created man looked at the heart of man. He was not interested in the outward appearance, but his actions. What man did was either pleasing or displeasing to God. I realized that I was looking to be accepted by my peers and the ones I came in contact with. I had missed the mark because God was more interested in the condition of my heart than at my appearance. My whole attitude changed. I did not have to waste my time seeking approval from those around me. The only one whose approval mattered was God.

The children were surprised at the way I had not only presented the lesson but the glow on my face as I explained the substance of the story. It was then that I explained to them the reactions I had received when someone had looked at my face. The whispers and comments had bothered me. I explained further that preparing this story had changed my attitude. I told them why my skin had patches and how it would probably get worse. I further explained that how I looked did not matter with God. What mattered was how I lived for Him. In giving me vitiligo, He did something special. I did not look like the normal people because I was special to God.

Those little kid's faces lit up, and during their recess they made sure their friends knew that their teacher Miss Patnaik was very special because God had allowed her to have a very special face. That day, instead of feeling sorry for myself and being angry with the situation, I had not only learned to accept it but also teach these little children not to look at life as a cup half empty but as a cup half filled. Life does have its ups and downs. It is what makes life interesting. How we handle it makes us strong. Even though I knew the characteristics of God, I had doubted Him and had put myself through pain and dejection because I failed to realize that God loved me. He had a reason for everything and would take me through this difficult situation, if I placed my trust in Him.

Though my attitude had changed, the appearance on my face continued to get worse. It did not bother me because I had learned to accept it, but it bothered my younger sister Rajini who was hurt and angry and ready to speak to the people who dared to hurt my feelings. It was strange, but even those who knew and worked with me treated me differently, but my students over the years and their parents loved and appreciated me.

A TEACHER WITH NEW PERSPECTIVE

I think this experience gave me a new perspective on how I looked at the children who were sent to my class. We had several kindergarten classes and three first grade classes. At the end of a school year, the kindergarten teachers got together and decided which first grade class each of the kindergarten children would be placed in. They tried to match the needs and personality of the child to the teacher.

We have to remember that in a class of 25 there would be at least a few who were exceptional children who were eager to learn and please the teacher. The majority of the children were those who worked hard and at the same time enjoyed themselves. But there was also a small group of children who were either less motivated, full of fun, or the ones who were not ready to be in that grade and seldom found interest in learning. They had to be challenged. I discovered that the last category of children fell between the cracks if they were not challenged to learn before they left the first grade. In schools like ours where the standard and expectancy was very high, a few of the children began to feel they did not belong in our particular school while they were still young. They seemed to have a chip on their shoulders and were not successful and sometimes had behavioral problems.

Having vitiligo and experiencing rejection made me understand and feel what it was like not being a part of the group that was not accepted by the majority. I understood what it felt like when someone stared at you or whispered amongst themselves when you passed by. I was like a nerd that no one wanted in their group. I understood why God had allowed me to go through this experience. He wanted me to show compassion to the ones who felt they did not belong to a certain class of people. God always has a reason for what He does. He was preparing me to be an advocate for the children who had missed the mark. No longer did I wonder why me. Why do I have to have a particular child who would be the reason for sleepless nights in my class? Instead, I was willing and excited to have the children who had been troublesome or had not been able to keep up with the assignments or those who hated to come to school. I wasn't trained in Special Education, but I loved and worked for a Master Teacher who was able to meet the needs of every child no matter what their individual needs might be. His name is Jesus and He had called me to teach. He loved the little children. In fact, when the disciples tried to send them away in Matthew 19:14, Jesus told them, *"Suffer little children and forbid them not to come unto me; for such is the kingdom of heaven."* I was not a reject of society, and neither were they. It was our duty as teachers to make time for them, the way Jesus had asked the children to come to Him even though he was tired. As teachers, we are asked to treat every child placed in our class with love and compassion.

Furthermore, I was called to teach not only the ones who were ready to learn but the ones who were not eager or felt they could not. What a calling! I vowed and prayed that with the help of my Master Teacher, every child in my class would not only accomplish their requirements but enjoy first grade and feel successful when they left. And I must say, they did. However, I do have to acknowledge it was not because of me but "Christ in me" that enabled these children to feel good about themselves. My parents supported me in everything I tried to do and also helped me in special art, cooking, science, or holiday projects I did with the children.

It was great to see the parents of the children who were struggling hold their heads high when their little ones got their certificate at the end of the school year. They certainly believed their children were capable and could accomplish greater things in the days that lay ahead. Their children were just like any other child and with a little encouragement and help would be successful, not a drop out.

I think seeing every child in their class be successful is the greatest reward that any teacher can ever ask for. It is a feeling that uplifts you even when times are difficult. Not only does the teacher see the difference in that child, but everyone else that comes into contact with that child does too. It enhances the confidence in the child who desires to do his/her best in the years that lie ahead. As a teacher, we have allowed the child to have a second chance in life. That is something that money can't buy but something God would expect of us who are called to be a teacher.

A LABOR OF LOVE

Produced From Our Garden

Mother carried on living her life as if nothing had happened. She still enjoyed working in her gardens. It is amazing the different kinds of vegetables she grew. Some of them grew in pots. For the first time in our lives we harvested potatoes, onions, and garlic. Neighbors envied us and said Mother had "Green Fingers." It was amazing the amount of vegetables she got not only from the small garden but from the flower pots. She was very proud of the contribution she made to our family dinner. Her labor of love was much appreciated, and it helped to keep her busy during those lonely hours. Rajini was so excited to see the purple potatoes Mother had harvested. She had brought some seedlings. Those potatoes were very expensive to buy, but now we had plenty of purple potatoes to enjoy without spending a penny.

Our neighbors could not believe the transformation Mother had brought to the barren, hard rocky piece of land that existed before we came. They could not believe a woman in her seventies had made all this difference with her bare hands. It looked beautiful! There were different kinds of roses, gladioli, dahlias, and other flowers. Our home was the only one that had such beautiful flowers. The dahlias were different shapes and colors. Some were huge while others were medium or small. We had every kind of rose including one called the Forty Niners. Our garden was so beautiful that it attracted much attention.

It reminded me of what the Lord could do with a life that was barren and fruitless if submitted to Him. "The touch of the Master's hand can and does change the worthless life just as mother's labor of love and hard work had changed the barren and worthless piece of land in the front and back garden and the house we lived in." I tell you, He changed my life and I am positive He can do it for you too.

One day a representative from the horticultural department in our community stopped by to admire the flowers. When she saw Rajini in the garden, she commented on the flowers and asked her to enter the dahlias in a contest at the San Mateo Fair. Rajini immediately replied that they were the product of our mother's hard work and unfortunately, she did not know English. She asked Rajini to enter the contest in her name, to which my sister replied that she could never take the credit for mother's hard work.

The only reason I mention this is to establish the fact that each one has been given gifts by Almighty God. Mother's gift was to use her hands to make her surroundings beautiful and her home well cared for. Mother did not complain of her loneliness. Instead she used her time and talents to make a house that had been an eyesore, to one that was admired and appreciated.

We too have been given gifts by God and all He desires of us is to make the best use of them. We are asked to be good stewards because one day we will have to give an account to our Heavenly Father. We can and should use the gifts we have received to bring joy into the lives of others and contentment to ourselves.

So, although Mother did not make a monetary contribution to the family, she did so through her hard work. She cooked and fed us with the freshest vegetables and fruit. Our table was always adorned with the most beautiful flowers, and the fragrance from the dishes she created stopped quite a few passers by.

Some people were shocked that our mother lived with us. They would never do it because of the added burden. Not so for us. Mother made our lives easier to live and enjoy. We never had to worry about the food we ate or the house we lived in and she never worried about what was in store for her because she not only enjoyed what she did but enjoyed every minute spent with us. We were blessed to have our mother and she was blessed to have us.

Our mother was a great influence on us. Although life was hard, with her encouragement we not only saved but we set aside money for our home improvement. Ever so often we found something that needed to be done. Although Mother had never mentioned it, she knew that our home could not compare to the wonderful homes each of our brothers and sisters had. Not only was it the smallest but it needed a great deal of improvement. We took her advice and within a few years our home had the best window dressings, hardwood floors, a beautiful enclosed deck, an open concept renovated kitchen with many cabinets, a laundry room, a master suite, and a den that had been converted from the garage. This also served as an extra living/bedroom when needed. I am glad we had listened to our mother. The house now looked beautiful on the inside as well as the outside. Our family and friends always knew there was a bedroom in our house that they could use if they visited. It made our mother proud of us and our home.

EXTENDED FAMILY

Once in a while we went over to Fresno to visit with Theophilus and Sonia. By this time both the girls Monica and Christina were married. Monica had moved to Southern California with her husband and son while Christina lived in Fresno with her husband and two children. They had a huge house and a large back and front yard where they had plenty of fruit trees and a beautiful garden with many kinds of vegetables. Later they moved to Oregon.

Although our mother never asked us to take her to Fresno, she was always excited when Rajini asked her if she wanted to visit her children and grandchildren. She loved seeing Theophilus, Sonia, Christina, and her husband and great grandchildren. Although the visits were short-lived, the time spent with her extended family brought great joy to her. She loved it and made the best of every moment. Imagine the excitement a mother must have had to see her children, grandchildren, and great-grandchildren all in the same place. The language barrier made no difference. We had a lot of fun even though we had to leave the next day to return home.

Besides visiting Fresno, we sometimes visited Conica and her children in Redding. Rajiv, her grandson, was in Southern California University while Ritika, her granddaughter, was finishing high school in Redding. Our mother's greatest joy was her grandchildren. She had missed being there when they were kids, but now she was glad she could see them once in a while. Her family was very important to her. They were doing well and had a home they could be proud of. She could not ask for anything more.

Since Kumila and her husband lived in Denver, Mother always looked forward to the time when they visited us or we visited them. Those were long happy days because we did not have to drive back the next day. We always waited until I had had a few days of vacation time. Even though we had to fly, it did not stop Mother from preparing special food that Kumila liked and freezing it so we could take it for Bis and her. She could not wait to surprise Kumila with all the goodies her hands had prepared. The week we spent just flew by because Kumila had arranged a variety of things she wanted to do with the family. It was an exciting time for us and always a sad time when we had to say good-bye.

I think one of the most exciting visits we had was on one Thanksgiving weekend. I think there had been an early winter in Denver. We realized this when we found that our flight had been cancelled due to a snow storm. We had to wait several hours before catching a flight to Denver. We were tired when we arrived at the airport but could not wait to arrive at their home. We were excited to see snow piled in front of their home. Though we went to bed late, we got up early the next morning. Of course, we could not resist the temptation of playing in the snow. We built a snowman complete with a hat, a carrot for his nose, branches for his hands, and Bis's scarf around his neck. It was a sight to behold, one that all of us enjoyed. The Thanksgiving dinner was an added blessing. That was one of our best Thanksgiving experiences we as a family ever had.

Mother was always excited when Kumila called to say she was going to visit us. Fortunately, the airport was very close to our home. Kumila had no problem taking the taxi from the airport if we were not available to meet her. On some occasions, Bis was able to join her and our little home was full of excitement as we enjoyed each other's company.

Even though Patricia lived so far away in Melbourne, Australia, Mother always looked forward to her visits. She made several trips to Calcutta and the USA, London and a trip to Europe and Thailand. Each of them was just as exciting as the one before. As usual, there was no end to our mother's joy when her eldest daughter visited. Even though she spent a lot of time with us, for mother, it seemed the days just flew by. She always wished her children's visit was for a longer time. She was very proud to introduce them to her neighbors and acknowledged she was a very fortunate mother to have children visiting her even when they lived so far away. This was one of the best gifts life had to offer her and she made a special effort to enjoy every moment she was with them.

Mother was very excited when we told her we were going to Australia to visit Patricia and Stuart. The journey was a long one, and the customs officers took their work very seriously. They would not allow Mother to take some chocolates she had bought for Patricia and Stuart. I think the officers saw Mother's sad face and told her she could take them only that time but not in the future visits she made. Mother was elated and could not resist her smile of gratitude. The days flew by quickly, but the time spent with family was worth it all. As always, saying good-bye was very difficult.

Mother always made time to stay in touch with the folks in Calcutta. She never forgot where she came from and always reminded them of the goodness and faithfulness of God. Not only did He bring her to America, but allowed her to be close to the family, visit India twice, vacation in Europe, England, Canada, and see a little of Bangkok. This was more than what she and Dad had expected and she could not understand why God was so good to her. I know it was because she and Dad had been faithful to God. They loved Him and served Him the best way they could. They depended on Him, worked hard, and trusted Him to make what was impossible possible. Such is our God who created us and wants the very best for us if we only trust Him and live according to His will. He will in His time make what is humanly impossible, possible. This does not mean we will travel to faraway lands like Mother did, but it does mean He will reward us in ways we could never imagine.

A Mother's Heart Breaks For The Third Time

Theophilus was always busy at his place of work, helping Sonia in the travel agency or fixing things at home. He even enjoyed cooking a meal or barbecue for the family. He loved to entertain, but as the days progressed, we noticed that he was not as energetic as before. He was not well. He went to the best doctors available and finally discovered his kidneys were not functioning well. He never missed an appointment nor his medication. They waited for a kidney donation, but the wait was futile. At first, Theo took everything in his stride as if nothing was wrong. He kept busy doing something or another hoping his health would improve. No matter what he or the doctors did, there was no improvement. His health was deteriorating and he seemed to give up hope.

Sonia, his wife, was determined not to give up and tried every avenue, doing her best to attend to him. She made sure she was there when Theo visited the doctor, which was quite often. Even though he was not as strong as before, it did not keep him off his feet. He kept busy despite his deteriorating health. His kidney was not functioning well so he went on dialysis. It was amazing to see how Sonia took care of his medical needs, and I am certain that with her diligence Theo managed to continue to live his life as well as he could. But he continued to get weaker and needed intensive medical care. He couldn't have asked for a better nurse than Sonia. She did everything she could to help him live a normal life, but soon realized he had to be admitted to hospital where Sonia then spent much of her waking hours. She wanted to make sure the doctors and nurses were able to attend to Theo's needs. She wanted to communicate with them on Theo's behalf. I am sure she hoped to see my brother return home, but nothing helped Theo to improve. Instead he seemed to get worse and less aware of his environment.

As if that was not bad enough, Mom's health was not too good either. She continued to ask the Lord to spare his life, but he was getting worse. We discovered that she was getting weaker and was also losing her appetite. We took her to her doctor frequently, but the doctor did not find anything wrong. She seemed lethargic and uninterested in the day-to-day activity. I think seeing her eldest son so sick was causing her great anxiety and she could not handle it.

You can imagine how it must have affected a mother. A few years earlier she had witnessed the burial of her youngest son and now her eldest was very sick and hospitalized. Without a kidney transplant, there seemed to be no hope. She wished she was closer so she could spend time with him. We visited him as often as it was possible, but that did not help to take away the pain that Mother was experiencing.

Although the doctors tried their best, Theo did not survive. We heard the awful news that Theo had gone to be with his Lord. We arranged to go to Fresno. This was the worst news Mother could get. She could not handle it. She practically collapsed. She had to be admitted into the hospital. We had already arranged to go to the funeral service but had to cancel. Mother was released the next day in the evening and was determined to attend the funeral service. The hotel reservation had been cancelled, but she would have none of it. She was going to Fresno even though she was unsteady on her feet. We immediately got ready and left. It was beginning to get dark, and the weekend rush was bad. We got to Fresno at midnight and discovered every hotel was booked because of a convention.

After trying several places, we decided to park outside a motel with their permission. We had barely got ready to relax in the car when the motel owner came running out to say he would cancel the last reservation since the person had failed to arrive before midnight. The room was ours if we still wanted it. We couldn't believe it. God knew that Mother was in no position to spend the night in the car. He not only provided us with a room, but it was the best one in the motel. It was huge, geared for a disabled family. God is good!

The next day we attended the funeral and the memorial service. Although it was a difficult time for our mother, she actually did better than we expected. She needed to say goodbye to her son, and God saw to it that it was possible. She was very quiet when we returned home. I can't imagine what must have gone through her mind, now that she had witnessed the burial of both her sons. We were glad that we had done everything possible to take her to Fresno.

The funeral actually helped our mother deal with her sorrow. It gave her comfort to see the grandchildren and great grandchildren. She felt very proud to hear people who knew and loved Theo say great things about him. I think she was glad I stood up and spoke on behalf of my mom and sister. She loved Theo and had much to say but could not because of the language barrier. But when I stood up and expressed her feelings, it made her feel good. Rajini and I were not too comfortable in taking Mom to Fresno in her condition. But I think we made the right decision. Mom needed to say goodbye and she needed to know how Theo had touched many lives.

We decided to leave immediately after the service because we had a long way to go and we wanted our mother to go to bed early. We were concerned for her. But I must say it was strange to see that Mother was actually feeling better than when we left on Friday evening, straight from her hospital bed. Although weak, she was able to take the four-hour trip back home reasonably well. We could not have done it without the help of God. I am glad Rajini was prepared to drive after a hard day's work, so late that Friday evening. God gave her the courage, took us to Fresno safely, and provided us with a good place to rest. It was worth it all. Mother needed to be there, and God saw to it that her desire was fulfilled. We were all very tired. We were glad we had stopped for dinner before we came home and were ready to rest our tired bodies.

The Loss Of A Son Takes Its Toll

Mother was now 82 years old. Although she didn't look her age, she did look tired and sad—especially when she did not know her daughters were watching. She tried to keep busy during those lonely hours while we were at work. She seemed to worry about losing us and waited at the window until we got home. She was so relieved when she finally saw us arrive. She looked and felt a little better and more relaxed. I can understand why she was so concerned to see us back home for the night. She had already lost three family members she loved and was very afraid of losing another one of her children. Unfortunately, we did not understand then, and sometimes got impatient with her. She was like a mother hen who could never relax until all her chicks were under her wings, safe for the night.

Apart from her concern for the two girls, she seemed to have lost interest in living. With this came the gradual loss of appetite and the excitement of preparing food for her family. We wondered if she was losing the desire to live. We talked to her about this and she insisted she just did not have an appetite.

One day we came home to find our mother very agitated. We wondered what had happened. As usual, Mother had gone out to the yard after her lunch and had accidently locked herself out. She did not know what to do and sat on the steps of the front door and waited for us to come home. That meant she had been sitting outside for almost four hours. She was all shaken up and wept her heart out when she saw me. Both Rajini and I were really worried and wondered what we could do.

There was no way we could give up our job and stay home with our mother. We needed every penny to pay the mortgage, the bills, and the day- to-day expenses. So we decided to visit our neighbor June who was already retired and always at home and asked if she would keep a set of keys for us. Mother was very comfortable with June and we knew she would be able to get the extra keys. She was willing to do this for us. So we left a set of keys with her and took Mother over and explained to her that June would help her get in if she needed assistance to open the doors. We were blessed to have three good neighbors who were very friendly and helpful. They had retired and all three of them loved our mother and assured us they would keep an eye on her. Our mother felt safe to be on her own now that she knew she could never be locked out. She felt confident to enjoy both the back and front yards and get help if and when she needed it.

Even though she was more relaxed to be alone, something had changed in Mom's behavior. As we observed her, we noticed that the dementia was getting worse. Mother seemed to forget little things and we worried about it. Rajini decided to take over the preparation of the meal when she came home after work. She did not want our mother to forget the food on the stove or forget to turn it off when she finished. Rajini enjoyed cooking and this was her opportunity to do what she liked doing best and at the same time make sure Mom was safe.

I made sure Mother had a good breakfast before I left for work and left her lunch in the microwave which she could warm when it was time for lunch. There was one other problem that we had to take care of. That was to make sure Mother was able to connect with us if she needed to do so. She could use the phone, but since both of us had to be connected by the operator, it was difficult for Mom to contact us due to language barrier. So, we made sure our respective bosses knew about this problem and we could then be connected if the need arose. This gave us some peace of mind.

One day while watching TV, we saw an advertisement for a medical alert which could be installed for a small monthly payment. It was available for people who needed help when alone. If there was an emergency, the one touch button connected her to the emergency department, her primary care doctor, and also notified the fire department and me. Even though our mother did not know English, they could have a three-way connection. It would get me on the phone to be a translator for my mother and the emergency department. The school I worked in was only about ten minutes away and I could come home if needed. The system would allow her to get help both in the house as well as the back and front yard. That meant Mother would have the freedom to be in the yard and still be able to call for help if necessary. This was a very good idea. Mother would be safe while we continued to work without unnecessary fear and distress of leaving Mother home alone.

We were very happy when Mrs. Sheley said it would be alright for me not only to take the call when it came but go home if it was necessary. I was fortunate to have a boss who was concerned for the welfare of my mother and was willing to allow me to go home if there was a need. So, we got the life alert installed and now Mother could wear the gadget around her neck and use it whenever it was necessary. You can't imagine how relieved Rajini and I felt. Even though we could not stay at home with Mom, we knew one of us would be right there if there was a need. It certainly made us feel happier to leave our mother home alone during the day. No longer did we feel guilty for not being home. Instead, we felt good that she would be taken care of no matter what the situation was.

Life was back to normal. We could see the relief on our mother's face. She could continue doing what she liked doing without any fear or trepidation. She had a caring neighbor who would unlock the door for her if she locked herself out and she would get immediate help if there was a need knowing full well one of her daughters would be available to help her in translating for her. We were comfortable to leave our mother home alone during the day as well as do our best at work.

A Dream Becomes A Reality

Mother Loved The Beach

A few days later, our mother came to me as I sat on the sofa and asked me if I would be willing to fulfill a dream that she had for me. She made me understand it would give her peace of mind. Wanting to grant her this desire, I told her I would do anything she asked. I wondered what it was and if I had made the right choice in saying I would grant her request.

Mother sat down near me and put her arms around me. Then with tears in her eyes, she told me that in her desire to see both her girls become self- sufficient and have a home for themselves, she had failed to be sensitive to my needs. She realized that I had put my interests on the back burner. She was aware that as a child I always wanted to receive the highest education possible. As a teacher it was appropriate for me to get my Master's and I hadn't because there were more important things to do to survive in America. So, before she died, she wanted to make sure that I had got my Master's. It would give her peace of mind. I tried to convince her that I had everything I needed and this was no longer a priority. Besides, I knew that working and taking care of our mother was a full-time job for both Rajini and myself. There was no free time during the day. (You see, by this time her health had deteriorated. There was very little she could do for herself.) Just to pacify her, I said I would think about it, but deep down in my heart I knew it was an impossible situation.

After we had taken care of our mother in the evening, I had to correct papers and prepare for the next day's class before I went to bed each night. Rajini on the other hand had to make sure our lunch and the dinner had been cooked and was ready for the next day. Besides these responsibilities, I had no computer skills whatsoever which would be a necessity if I considered keeping the promise I had made to my mother. Frankly, I tried not to think about it, knowing it was unlikely to happen. I hoped somehow Mother would forget she had asked me to keep that particular promise.

Even though my mother was not in the best of health, she did spend time each day with the Lord. She read her Bible and spent a lot of time praying for each of her children and her extended family. I know she was praying for the doors to open so I could get my Master's degree. I know this was true because a few days later a strange thing happened.

After our morning devotions, the teachers were given a flier which stated that it was possible for us to get a Master's degree if we were willing to attend classes one evening a week and two Saturdays a month when instructions and assignments would be given. Most of the work had to be done through independent study. We would be graded on the tests and special assignments. The administrators and superintendent of our school encouraged their teachers to register because it would not only be good for the accreditation of the school but would enable the teachers to get a higher salary when we graduated with a Master's degree. That was so tempting. To my amazement, God had answered my mother's prayers! We could work at our own pace and finish it when we desired. I knew that in my case it had to be sooner rather than later because of the condition of my mother's health. It meant that I had to complete my studies before the end of the second year. I knew this was humanly impossible. I had no computer skills necessary for turning in my assignments and had very little free time. I did not know how I could explain all this to my mother before the deadline for registration.

I prayed for guidance. Being a failure had never been an option. I had to make a decision and I knew what that would be. I could not let my mother down; I took a step of faith and submitted my application. Mother was thrilled to hear of it and was glad the Lord had answered her prayers.

For days I struggled with the promise I had made to my mom and wondered how I would fulfill it. I knew it was going to be very difficult. Both Rajini and I had a great deal to accomplish before we went to bed. Besides that, I had to make sure that mother was in bed before 10 p.m. Then I would be free to learn how to work on a computer, study, and also do my assignments. Fortunately, Rajini was already used to working on the computer at work and we had a computer at home. She taught me the basics, but I can assure you I was a very bad student where the computer was concerned. I forgot to save the little I did, each time I left the desk. Which meant that I had to redo my first few assignments for several days. If I wanted to graduate by the projected time, I would have to turn in all my assignments on the due date and pass every test. I had very little sleep, little time, and much to accomplish.

Fortunately, I had the Lord on my side, and I was amazed that even with very little sleep and a big workload, a giant huddle could be crossed. It was not easy, but God gave me the strength and the wherewithal to take care of Mom, teach, correct all my student's assignments, prepare, and complete all my assignments on time. I was not too happy with a few of my test results, but I averaged out well.

The most difficult time for me was the end of each quarter at school. Added to the daily requirements we had to get the progress report for each child in, the grade book completed and the report card for the administrator to sign. This was really stressful. Somehow, I managed it all in a timely manner.

Normally I worked summer sessions at school every year. This always helped me to make extra money to go on short vacations with my family. But this year because of classes and assignments to complete, I decided not to work. This gave me extra time and confidence to know there was a possibility to graduate by the projected time. Towards the beginning of summer vacation, the three of us who had decided to graduate hired a young lady who had just graduated from high school. She was fast at typing and excellent on the computer, and knew how to present the final written assignments in the format required. We had a week to submit it.

Each one of us had a different assignment to submit. Since it was summer vacation, most of the classrooms were empty and we were able to work on our individual assignments. When we were ready and had typed it up, we gave it to the young lady who then typed it in the format required. This was a blessing. I was the last to finish and held my breath as the clock ticked by. It was late in the evening and the final day for my papers to be mailed in was the very next day. True to her word, my assignment was ready to be submitted. What a relief!

We had one more assignment where we had to submit at least 38 pages with a Table of Contents and a Bibliography on "Scripture and God & Senior Theology." It was due a few weeks later.

This was a very difficult assignment. Pastor Al Franklin had taught us thirteen main topics over the period of our attendance. Fortunately, I had taken the time to study and write my thoughts on each topic each time it had been taught. I still had to find books of several theologians who wrote on those topics. Then I had to find materials from those books to substantiate my thoughts and ideas. In the short weeks that were left, I had to read those books before I could start typing this paper.

Reading was something I always enjoyed. I had a variety of books in my personal library. When I looked at the books I had collected, I found I had in my possession, a number of books written by several theologians. This was good news. I did not have to go to a library; I had the books I needed. Reading each of these books was time consuming, but once I had started, I was able, with the help of God, to find everything I was looking for.

Since I was on summer break, I was more relaxed and had extra time on my hands. My computer skills had improved. I actually had more confidence and with the help of the Lord, I was able to tackle this assignment. Fortunately, the rough outline I had made ahead of time made it easier to do this specific assignment.

Once I started, it seemed as if every word fell into place like it needed to. I moved from one chapter to the next with very little difficulty. My mom and sister were very encouraging and just left me alone to complete my work. My mother had great faith that I would complete all my assignments on time. Every day seemed to bring me closer to the end. I even had enough time to re-read my finished assignment a few times and make the corrections I needed to make.

Then, just a few days before the due date, I had it all stapled and ready to mail. What a relief! I could relax and enjoy the last few days of my summer vacation. I had done my best and God would do the rest.

Summer vacation was finally over, and a new school year had started. I patiently waited for my results. I tried not to show it, but every day I eagerly looked for the mail to see if there was a special delivery for me. By this time, I was beginning to get very anxious when it finally arrived. I eagerly tore open the envelope to see if I had passed. To my surprise, I found I had done quite well. I could honestly say it was a team effort. The Lord was my greatest helper. My mother was my prayer warrior and my sister was there, not only to help me with the computer but do extra housework so I could finish my assignments. And we did it!

My greatest reward was to see our mother's face all lit up. Was this the same lady who for the past few months seemed to get more lethargic as the days went by? She seemed to be a new person. She was on the phone calling her few friends and telling them of my achievement. For her it was a big deal. Although my parents had very little education, they had prayed fervently that we, their children, would have every opportunity to get the education we needed and their prayers had been answered.

Rajini and Mother were very happy for me. They bought me a new dress and took me away for the weekend to celebrate. Mother did not feel very strong, but she made every effort to enjoy the occasion. God had granted her last request and she was happy.

God is good.

Joy Turned To Sorrow

Getting my Master's made a great difference in my paycheck. I thought about the time I had come to America without a penny in my pocket. Then I thought of the first paycheck I had received when I worked in the Bible bookstore. I remembered how I had struggled as I thought of my tithe for that Sunday. I remembered the Lord had reminded me that if I learned to give with a willing joyful heart, He would fill the barn till it overflowed. God was not a debtor. He did not need my money. He owned the universe and everything in it. He wanted me to have the right priority in my life. He wanted me to understand that everything I possessed was given to me by Him. Now, as I looked at my paycheck, it confirmed that same fact that God does not lie. He keeps His word when we do what is expected of us.

I am so glad that I gave in that day because I was a winner. Sometimes in our finite mind, we think giving our lives to Christ and obeying Him means we have to give up what we want. I learned that trusting God in everything means we acknowledge that He is supreme and is a caring, loving father who has our best interest in mind and will never withhold the best for His child. Trusting is difficult, but it is worth it if we do.

Now that I had completed my Master's, Mother felt that everything she had asked for from the Lord had been granted. She seemed disinterested in the daily activities. She was anxious to see us come home, but the joy she had of sharing the evening meal with her girls was no longer there. We knew there was something wrong, but her doctor insisted there was nothing the matter. She seemed so unconnected. A few weeks later, I received a letter asking me if I would like to attend the graduation service or get my diploma by mail. Mother was not strong enough to go to Redding, and we could not leave her alone at home. I was excited because it would have been my first graduation service. The university in India did not have a special graduation service to give out diplomas to the graduates. We were asked to pick it up. But now I had no choice; even though I longed to attend, I decided to ask for my diploma to be mailed.

Thanksgiving and Christmas were always an exciting time for us. We looked forward to celebrating both. Unfortunately, that was not the case this year. Rajini put a fantastic spread on the decorated Thanksgiving table, but Mother hardly participated in the celebration or ate anything. We did the best we could to have a fun time, but it was not the same.

For Christmas, Rajini arranged for us to have dinner at a fine restaurant in the city. I know I was excited. I helped Mother wear her finest and we set out in the car. Mother sat in her usual place, right in front near Rajini who was driving. Normally, Mother enjoyed talking as she looked at the city lights. But that day she was quiet for a while and then asked to be taken home because she felt very sick. Much as we hated it, we decided to return home. We were very disappointed. Rajini had not cooked for that evening meal. She found some leftovers, heated them, and we ate our dinner with a very heavy heart.

OUR GREATEST REGRET

We could not understand what was happening to our mother. I continued to take her to the doctor every week, but he insisted there was nothing wrong with her. He prescribed more medicine and asked her to drink more water. Like a fool I accepted what the doctor told me. Rajini and I could not understand what was going on and kept requesting mom to make an effort to eat, but she did not have an appetite nor the desire to eat. Something was definitely wrong, but we could not fathom what it was.

Now that I look back, I think I should have put all her symptoms into the computer and I am sure I would have gained some inkling of what was really going on. Instead, we believed the doctor and continued to wonder if our mother was imagining her pain and discomfort. We did everything to make her feel comfortable. We even tried to get a visiting nurse to come in for a few hours a day to help her. But finding one we could afford was just impossible. A few months later, we noticed she was losing weight and disinterested in everything, including her two girls. That was when I decided to sleep on the second bed in her room. In that way, I could keep an eye on her and help her if she needed it.

A few months later, when I got up during the night to check on Mom, I noticed she did not respond to me. She was breathing, but apart from that she did not even open her eyes. We called 911 and told them about Mom and the fire department came immediately. They tried everything, but my mother did not respond. The first responders arrived and immediately took her vitals and decided to take her to the nearest hospital. I am very thankful to the first responders who tried their best to attend to their patient and keep her comfortable and alive. The driver of the ambulance tried his best to comfort and assure me that everything would be fine even though he knew this was not so. I must say the first responders are extraordinary people. Not only do they give over and above what is required of them, they bend over backwards to do their best to encourage the family also. I knew all was not well with my mother, but I sure appreciate the encouragement I was given.

Although the hospital was not too far away, it seemed ages before we got there. We saw no improvement in the way my mother looked. The doctors and nurses immediately attended to her and did their best to find the problem. Very soon they discovered that our mother's sugar level had gone beyond the limit and their patient was in a coma. I was shocked. How did that happen? It could not have happened overnight. We had done our best to take her to the doctor practically every week and her doctor had convinced us there was nothing wrong. We were never told she was diabetic or her sugar level was not normal.

It was already morning, and Rajini had come as fast as she could. She was shocked to hear that our mother was in a coma and in intensive care. There was nothing we could do. I convinced her to go to work and called in to say I could not be at work that day.

Even though Mother had been in ICU for two days, we saw no changes. The doctors and nurses in America are trained to give every patient their best. They do everything possible for the patient until there is nothing more to be done. Our mother was still in a coma. They assured me that our mother would be in intensive care for a while and they would inform me if there was any change. Seeing there was nothing Rajini and I could do, we continued to go to work. The hospital was only a short distance away from the school, so I could be there within fifteen minutes if there was a necessity. We made sure I was there every morning before work to check on Mother and every evening both of us were there after work for a few hours.

This was a very difficult time for us. Mother had been in hospital for almost two weeks before, but it was nothing like this. Previously I had spent the night with my mother on a couch. The only time our mother was alone was when I went to work. I was there to help her the rest of the time. It had been difficult to see her lying on her bed, but we could at least communicate with our mother, which was worth it all. It was gratifying to see her smile and hear her concern for us and the endless instructions she had for us. Now it was different. There seemed to be a blank look on her face and no response. We had faith God would heal her but had doubts she would ever be able to come home again or if she would be normal when she came out of the coma. Although we saw Mother for a short time every day, we saw no change at all for several days. We knew the doctors and nurses were doing their best and God would do what was best for mother. All we could do was wait and that was difficult.

WAITING IS NOT EASY BUT NECESSARY

The Bible instructs us in Psalm 27:14 *"Wait on the Lord; be of good courage, and He shall strengthen thy heart: wait I say on the Lord."* I knew this verse from memory and I understood what it meant. I am sure I had advised others to do so when they were desperate for an answer, but now I was the one who needed to be reminded of that verse. Seeing our mother lying there without any response and expression confirmed in our hearts that waiting was probably in vain. It is easy to quote the scripture to others and wonder why they cannot wait on the Almighty God for an answer. Honestly, even though we tried, the longer we waited the less confidence we had that Mother would be back to normal.

But one day when I arrived at the hospital, Mother was awake and aware of her surroundings. She was still too weak to be moved from the intensive care unit, but she was responding and it made Rajini and myself elated that she had awoken at last as if it were from a long sleep.

A day later, they moved Mother to a room close to the nurse's desk. It was good to see our mother's reaction when she saw us. This was great. It probably meant she would be ready to go home. We tried to get her appetite back with Rajini's good cooking, but even though she did her best to entice our mother to eat, it did not help. She seemed to want to do so but only ate a little which was understandable. All she was interested in was to know when she was going home. We tried to assure her that she would be home the moment the doctor was confident she was ready to go home. We wanted to cherish every moment that we could with our mother. So, I was there before I went to work to make sure the nurse was aware of any changes that Mother had experienced during the night. Rajini went home, before she came to the hospital with our evening meal for both of us. It gave our mother great joy to see her girls eat. We spent some time chatting with her and assured her she would be home as soon as she was released. She believed us and was confident that she would be going home in a few days.

While she was recuperating, our mother had developed a worse problem. It seemed that she was not only diabetic but had hyperglycemia. The sugar level was never stable. It was either too high or too low and had to have constant care. When I went to visit my mother, I was asked by the nurse at the station to go to the office. I was told that my mother needed special care either at home or at the nursing home where her glucose level could be monitored and immediate action be taken to prevent any further medical concerns. Both my sister and I could not stay home and did not have the ability to meet her medical needs. We wanted our mother to have the best care but could not do it ourselves. I was asked to take time to think about and set up a meeting with the Social Services.

I met with the representative a day later. She told us we had two options available for our mother. We could take her home and take care of her or hire someone to do so or she could be taken to the nursing home where she would be cared for.

I came home that day with a very heavy heart. We loved our mother and wanted to bring her home where she belonged. We knew there was no cure for her latest condition. She needed someone to keep a careful eye on her and make sure her blood sugar was in control at all times. We had to make a decision soon. The only option we had was to put her into a nursing home where we hoped she would get the best care. So much against our desire, we allowed the hospital to transport our mother to the nursing home closest to our home where we hoped she would get the quality care she needed. I drove behind the emergency vehicle to the nursing home and got our mother admitted in. Then I called Rajini and let her know the details. Unfortunately, our mother thought she would be there for a short while. She was positive she would get strong soon and return home.

Both of us stayed with our mother until close to ten o'clock. We made sure Mom was aware of her surroundings and knew how she could get help if she needed it. We met the nurses and their aides to make sure that they would care for our mother. We convinced ourselves that she was in good hands. This was a big adjustment for Mom. She was in a semi-private room. The other bed that day was empty, but the room was right next to the nurse's station. We prayed with our mother, and after we had kissed her, we assured her we would be there for her. We waited with our mother as long as we could and then we had to leave.

Both of us were very quiet. We felt we had deserted our mother when she needed us most. We felt we had made the wrong decision. We had promised our mother we would bring her home but knew that was probably not possible. We were also aware that very few inmates at her age and in her condition ever left the nursing home. We decided to spend most of our available time with our mother. It would be difficult but possible if we tried.

In keeping with our decision to be with our mother as much as we could, both of us took on individual responsibilities. I was very fortunate that I was close to both the nursing home and work. So, I volunteered to go to the nursing home every morning before work to make sure all was well with Mom during the night and encourage her. I made sure she understood I was only a phone call away. Then I went straight to school to be with my students who were so caring and tried to be on their best behavior. I did all my corrections and preparations for school during my free time and rushed after school to be with my mother. Even though I tried to convince her that this arrangement was only for a short time, she was not convinced I meant a word I said.

Spending time with our mother was very precious. I shared with her all that had happened at home and at school as I wheeled her around in the nursing home. She waited patiently for Rajini to come. It was a long wait because Rajini would go home and bring our dinner with her. Then when Rajini came, we ate together in her room. This was a special time for the three of us. Strange as it may seem, it gave my mother great joy to have her dinner with her girls. It also assured her that we were taking care of ourselves and eating well. After a short devotion, we got her ready for bed, assured her we would see her the next day, and drove home.

On arriving home, Rajini cooked the meal for the next day and I did the housework, and got ready for bed. Rajini always left home by ten minutes past five in the morning to catch the bus on the main street. But before she left, she made sure we had breakfast and our lunch was ready to take to work. We had to keep healthy and strong, so we could carry out all our responsibilities.

It was amazing to see how God gave us the strength we needed for the day and the courage to face the situation he had placed us in. Even though these were difficult times, we considered it our privilege to be available for our mother in her time of need. She had given her best for us, even when it was very difficult. Her needs were always forgotten so she could take care of us and our needs. Now it was our turn to give of our time and energy to attend to her needs and God would help us. Of that we were sure.

Visiting our mother at the nursing home taught me a few important facts. As I wheeled my mother around every day, I was surprised to learn there were close to 90 patients in the home. Most of them were seniors who had been brought there straight from the hospital. As usual, I stopped to say hello and introduce my mother to them. I noticed something quite unusual. Most of these residents did not seem to have any visitors, even on weekends or on special holidays. Some of them had no visitors or mail at all during their entire stay. (And we wonder why some residents fall between the cracks!) For me it was heart-breaking.

There was one particular lady who kept watch for my sister and I to visit our mother. She stopped me one day while I was on my rounds visiting the women. She made a remark that I will never forget. She said and I quote, "Your mother is a very lucky woman." I told her it was the contrary. We were very fortunate to have her. She told me that I did not understand what she meant. She informed me she had been in the nursing home for several months and she had not received even a letter or phone call from her daughter who was her only child. From her purse she took out a picture of a beautiful young lady. It was all she had to remember her daughter with.

How could such a thing be possible when it did not cost even a penny to make a call? Surely, none of us are so busy that we are unable to call a loved-one, even on a special occasion like a birthday, Christmas, or on Mother's Day. What has this world come to? That day I made up my mind that I would make sure the little kids in my class would be taught the importance of "Keeping in Touch," not only with a loved-one but with those God brought us into contact with.

The Forgotten Group

The 4 Girls Visiting Mother at The Nursing Home

We thought Mother was settling down and beginning to show signs of improvement. She was longing to go home and hoped it would be soon. One day when I came to visit her, I noticed she had packed all her things and was waiting to go home. She looked excited. When I checked with the nurses, they assured me that they had not told her anything about going home. You should have seen the disappointment that set in when I told our mother that I could not take her home unless her doctor said she was doing fine and gave me permission to do so.

All the joy seemed to go from her face. She promised she would not be a burden to us if we took her home. I tried to explain that she has never been a burden to us. Instead it was a joy to have her home. She was the reason why we had been successful and had such a beautiful home to live in. It was a very difficult situation for us to deal with. You see she could not understand how ill she was and the reason she needed individual care. Besides, her dementia seemed to be getting worse. She could never be left alone at home with dementia and poor health.

Unknown to us, a few days earlier she had been told that she would never go home and that the nursing home would be her new home. She was made to understand that the nursing home was where she needed to be and that she had to think of it as her new home. I think this confirmed in her mind that she was never going home because we did not want her home.

Going to the nursing home every day taught me a big truth that I had taken for granted. Sure, I loved my mother and appreciated her a great deal, but there was more to it.

I never considered how important it was for us to have our mother and for her to have us. My sister and I enjoyed visiting Mother and tried our best to make those few hours we spent with her count, but it was difficult. We knew there was a change. Our mother had accepted the fact that she was probably never going home and seemed to have lost the enthusiasm with which she greeted us every day. It felt as if we had lost the mother we knew and cherished. We tried to lift her spirit talking about all the activities of the day at the nursing home and at work, but it did not help. I doubt if she even heard anything we said. Thanksgiving came and went, but nothing we tried to do helped to brighten her day. The only time she seemed to be alert was when we shared the Bible reading and prayed with her.

Normally by the first day of December, the children at school were very excited. Almost every conversation was about celebrating Christmas. In our class we always did a few special projects, which included cards and gifts for their parents. We also made a special booklet with the entire Christmas story, which was illustrated with verses from the Bible. The intention was that the children would know the reason for celebrating Christmas. This year I felt compelled to do something special to bring joy to others. I wanted my children to show love to the less fortunate. I believe the residents in the nursing home needed cheering up during Christmas.

So, I spoke to the lady in charge of arts and crafts and asked her if it would be acceptable for the first graders of our school to make Christmas cards for each of the residents. She was elated and acknowledged that such a thing had never happened before and would be greatly appreciated. I was excited and shared this plan with the other two first grade teachers. They agreed it would make a good project for

Christmas. The children would be supplied with the paper and they could use their crayons, colored pencils, or paints and stickers to create Christmas cards after they finished their class assignments each day.

The children were very excited, and some of them even finished three cards while others did only one. Each card was one of a kind, and they all looked beautiful. Christmas vacation would start in two weeks, and I was so happy that I had over 90 cards before school closed.

I took the cards to the nursing home, which were distributed by the staff. I could not believe the amount of joy it brought to each of those residents. It was a big surprise and the best thing they had received. To know that someone cared enough to actually make a card for them was beyond their imagination. It had changed the atmosphere in that nursing home. Every table in every room had their individual cards displayed for all to see. It reminded me that anything done from the heart to express the love of the Lord would bring joy to the one who received it. It was extra special because the children had taken the time to make each one individually.

OUR LAST CHRISTMAS TOGETHER

For our mother, the fact that Christmas was drawing near made no difference. She had changed. She seemed resigned to just being there. She ate very little and said very little. To her the joy of living was gone. We did everything to cheer her up, but nothing made any difference. We began to understand that we were losing our mother a little every day. She was no longer interested in our daily activities or the news of the day. As Christmas drew near, there was excitement in the air. The residents looked forward to all the celebrations and special meals, but there was no excitement for our family.

I was on Christmas vacation and spent all day with my mother until Rajini joined us after work. I tried to get our mother excited about all the special activities at the nursing home. The residents were excited, but our mother seemed disinterested. I made sure she was there, but she was not too excited about it. We decided to have a family celebration by ourselves.

Rajini had planned a beautiful dinner and brought it with her. We managed to get a table in the dining room on which we put a beautiful tablecloth and a vase with flowers. We were determined to share a good family meal. Much as we tried, our mother seemed to have no appetite. She ate nothing. We ate our dinner, cleaned up, spent some time with her, and then went home.

As the days passed by, we realized that our mother's health was deteriorating. I was still on my Christmas vacation. I decided I would blend the food Rajini made and see if we could get our mother to drink it. It seemed to work for a few days. It gave her some strength, but she spent most of her days in bed.

The New Year came, and everybody was celebrating while we sat with our mother, fearing what the New Year had in store for us. Mother hardly spoke and never left her bed. Much as we tried, we could not get her attention. We still prayed with her, but there was no response.

We wondered if Mother could hear what we read and prayed. So I lay beside her as I read the Bible and prayed with my lips very close to her ears. She seemed to respond, though it was not verbal at all. In our minds we knew our mother was slowly slipping away. There was nothing anyone could do for her.

A TEST OF TRUE LOVE

We continued to visit our mother and tried to make conversation with her even though there was no response. The nurses could not get her to take her medicine. Then one day I received a call from her doctor while I was still at work. I knew it could not be good news. The doctor told me that my mother had not eaten for two days. They needed my permission to feed her through intravenous. I knew I could not do that because my mother and I had had a serious conversation a few years earlier. She made me promise that when it was time to meet her Lord and she was unable to eat on her own, I would not allow the doctor to make her live by using intravenous or by resuscitating her. It wasn't difficult then to translate that request of hers to her doctor while I sat in his office. She wanted to die a normal death. But now that the request needed to be carried through it was very difficult for me to allow the doctor to do what my mother had requested. At the time of her request, I had several brothers and a sister older than me, but she did not want anyone to dispute her request. She wanted me to take care of her desire. I agreed and took her to her doctor and allowed him to record her request. I translated what she said as the doctor recorded it. Then he had my mother sign it before it could be put in her personal file.

Now it was different. Mother was no longer able to talk for herself, and I was responsible for making that decision. I had to tell the doctor not to put feeding tubes into my mother's body. It was difficult to carry through with the decision I had signed up for years ago. I loved my mother. I could not pull the plug on my own mother. I needed time and told the doctor I would think it over and be in his office later with my answer. I had to get back to my class and a decision had to be made.

The office secretary arranged for someone to take my class and asked Dr. Sheley, the pastor of the church and owner of the school, to talk and pray with me so I could make the right decision. Pastor Sheley left everything on the table and immediately came down to meet with me. He started with a prayer seeking God's guidance and wisdom. I remember the first thing he asked me when I had explained why I needed to meet with him. He said, "Do you love your mother and how much do you love her?" Immediately I replied that I loved her enough to give my life to see her survive. He assured me that seeing her survive was what I wanted. My wish to keep her alive was my desire. If I really loved her, I should honor her request and grant her heart's desire. She had chosen and had trusted me enough to let me handle her last request. She was ready to meet her Lord, and if He decided to take her, she should be able to accept it. She did not ask for resuscitation or feeding with the help of a tube. He told me to allow her the dignity to die a natural death. He was very gentle as he spoke with me and let me think about what he had said. Then he asked if he could pray for me and ask God to give me the direction I needed to take. It was a very moving prayer and I was thankful he made himself available even though he was in the midst of preparing the message for Sunday.

It Takes Courage To Do
What Is Right

I left the Pastor and went to my classroom. I was at peace, knowing what I needed to do but greatly disturbed that I was the one who had to make this critical discussion, one that would probably haunt me for the rest of my life. Somehow, I continued with my teaching. My students knew that something had happened to their teacher. I was always there to meet them in the playground to bring them in after lunch recess. I wasn't there that day. Children are very sensitive when it concerns someone they love. They were extra caring and very quiet. They did everything they needed to do, wondering what was wrong and how they could help. School was soon over. I dismissed the class and got ready to go to the doctor's office.

I had been to his office often, but this time it was different. I had to let him know my ultimate decision. I hardly took note of the traffic around me. My mind was in turmoil. I knew what had to be done, but was it the right thing to do? Would I regret it later, or worse still, would my family be upset for making such a decision? I wished I had not been given such a difficult responsibility. These thoughts continued to bother me, but before I knew it, I had arrived at the doctor's office. There was no escape. Difficult as it was, I had to do the right thing by my mother. I had to honor her request and give her the dignity of life.

I locked my car and slowly walked towards the doctor's office. The nurse immediately let him know of my arrival. He met me in his office and waited for my decision. It seemed I was tongue-tied. Not a word came out. Instead I burst into tears. He tried to explain the situation Mother was in and that immediate action had to be taken. I tried to tell him that he knew what Mother had requested. He agreed he did, but I had to formally request it again because I had been there to witness my mother's request. There was no getting out of it; I had to make the ultimate decision before he could fulfill mother's request.

With a burst of tears, I told him not to put tubes in and allow Mother to die a natural death as she requested. So, I signed the document giving permission to let Mother die a normal death. As I write this, tears start flowing down my cheek. I could see myself giving the doctor permission not to prolong my mother's life. I hope a time will come when I can talk about this without feeling guilty. It was Thursday, and the doctor explained that since no medicine could be given to our mother, she would be under the care of hospice. I needed to go to the nursing home the next day and meet with the representative at 12:00 p.m. She would tell me what the process would be. So I went to the nursing home to be with my mother.

The next day, during my lunch break, I decided to go to the nursing home and discover what hospice was all about. Mother had been moved to a different room where she had more privacy. I was met with the representative. She sat on a chair close to my mother's bed. It was strange to see Mom lying on the bed so peacefully. She seemed to be content. I shook hands with our guest and asked her what she had done to make our mother look so at ease considering they had a language barrier between them. The lady explained to me that her job was to be with her patient, talk to her in her soft voice, assure her that she would not be forced to take medicine or eat and drink anything she did not want. She was there to make sure she was comfortable. I could actually see a smile on Mother's face as our guest spoke to me.

This was strange. Somehow, she knew her wish had been carried out and she was content. I am glad I took the time to meet with her. It was worth it all. I was told that to make Mother more comfortable, they would be bringing in a very special bed for her. She told me her job would start on Tuesday because Monday was Dr. Martin Luther King's birthday which was a national holiday. Before she went, she gently rubbed Mother's hand and told her she would be there on Tuesday. Mother seemed to understand her and gave a smile in return and our guest left. I had to return to school. So, I prayed with my mother and went on my way.

I actually felt slightly better as I drove back to school and my students. I had seen a big difference in our mother since my last visit yesterday. Nobody had forced her to take her medicine or eat her food, yet she looked better for it. Pastor was right. In her mind, I had followed through with her request even though it was the most difficult decision I had to make. It did not mean that Mother would live for a longer period of time, but it did mean she would live better during her remaining time on Earth. In my mind, I knew that there was no doubt that our mother was here for only a short stay. Thankfully it was a three-day weekend, so I had time to deal with all the preparations like the funeral parlor, the plan for the grave, a casket, and the service.

I went back to school and faced my precious children. They were very quiet and concerned for me. They did not know what was happening, but they knew something was wrong. I could not have asked for a better set of children. They were quiet and very careful not to cause any problem for their teacher. It seemed that they actually understood their teacher was going through some pain of her own. Two hours later, I dismissed the class and was on my way to the cemetery close by to see what the process for getting a plot was. And then I went to the nursing home to be with our mother.

FINAL PREPARATION

Even though it was Saturday the next day, I decided to skip visiting my mother for a short while. Instead I went to the funeral parlor to find out what preparations I needed to make in advance. The gentleman was kind enough to guide me through the process. He told me I had to decide and pay for a plot in advance if I needed an option for a weekend burial. Then I had to meet with the pastor and arrange for the services.

Fortunately, at Kumila's previous visit we had already decided on the type of coffin we needed to get for our mother. So that was one thing off my list. There was so much more to do, and I continued to wonder if my decision would be acceptable by the rest of the family. I realized for the first time that I had to be strong and do the best I could even though it was a painful task to perform. It is amazing the way God helps in situations like this. He steps in and guides when all else seems to collapse around you. I did not realize there was so much to prepare for, and everything came with a heavy price. Fortunately I was in America where I could purchase anything with a credit card. I was sure the rest of the family would step in to help with the finance. All I knew was that my sister Rajini and I were determined to do everything we could possibly do to make "Mother's Homecoming Special."

It was Saturday. Rajini went to the nursing home to spend time with our mother while I decided to start taking care of all that needed to be done. At the funeral parlor, I met with the director who walked me through the process. He told me I had to purchase a plot first. So I drove to the cemetery and met with the representative who showed me the plots that were available. The cost of each plot depended on where it was situated. For the first time, I realized that funeral arrangements were not that easy. After seeing several plots, I chose the one nearest to the office and decided to complete the paperwork on Monday after we had discussed it at home.

We spent the rest of the day with our mother. She looked rested and more alert although she had nothing but a little water to drink.

She seemed pleased to see us but said very little. The weekend passed by without any further change, though something had changed for my sister and myself. There was no rush to get things done or eat our meal and there was hardly any conversation between us. It seemed that "silence was bliss." I think in our minds we had concluded that our mother was only there physically. She was ready to bid farewell to her earthly life and was just waiting for the Lord to take her home.

So we had decided on the plot we needed to purchase and then spent Sunday sitting by our mother's bedside. Thankfully Monday was a holiday for Dr. Martin Luther King's birthday, which allowed me to close the deal with the cemetery director. Rajiv, our nephew, had arrived from London and Rajini took him to visit our mother. Just as I had finished signing the paperwork and made the payment, I got a desperate call from Rajini. Mother had been called home. I could not believe it. I was working so hard to make time to visit with our mother. But she was gone before I said my good-bye.

I was broken, but there was no time to think of myself. There was much to do. Thank goodness I had already made arrangements with the funeral parlor to transport the body when the time came for them to do so. I had to call our mother's primary care doctor and let him know. Now it dawned on me. Planning for the funeral arrangement in advance was not an accident. It was within the plan of our Almighty God. He knew what I needed to do and prompted me to do so. The timing was just right. I could take care of everything else during the next few days. The only regret I had was that I had not said my farewell to my mother. I wished I had been there.

Absent In The Body Present With The Lord

Mom's Funeral

mmediately I rushed to the nursing home and was shocked to see our mother lying there with a smile on her face. I think she had waited patiently for this day when she would be united with our Lord and reunited with our dad and our brothers who had gone home before her. What a reunion that must have been and what a relief from all the pain she had been through in the last few years, but was it the same for us? One would say that it should have been a relief but not for the two of us. Mother had been a part of our lives from the day we had arrived into this world until today. She had been there through thick and thin, and now there was an empty space in our hearts and home. She had been the pillar in our home and life, and now she had gone to a better place, a place our Lord has prepared for those who love Him. We rested in the hope that one day we too would be welcomed home by our Lord where we will have the joy of meeting our parents and the rest of the family. But for now, we felt lost without her. I wished I had been there before she left this earthly home, but I had responsibilities to take care of and I am glad they were done.

There was so much to do and no time to grieve. We had decided to give our mother the best funeral and memorial service we could give, and there was much to do before that could happen. I decided to call the Pastor and make an appointment with him to arrange the service at the funeral parlor, the funeral service, and the memorial service at the church after the funeral. There was so much to do and so little time. Then Rajiv and I went to the funeral parlor to meet with the director to arrange the service for Thursday evening.

Unfortunately, for me, I had to go back to work for the next three days. As a teacher, we were allowed to take only three days off for bereavement, and I planned to take it later when I could spend time with my family. In a way that was good because it kept me busy. It helped me to carry on with my responsibilities and did not give me much time to think of the events I had to deal with. After work, I went with my nephew to meet with the Pastor and the music director to arrange for the three services. We also went to the funeral parlor to make the arrangements for the service on Thursday evening. Rajini stayed home to make the meals for the family and take care of the responsibilities at home.

Patricia from Australia and Kumila and Bis from Denver arrived within the next two days. The rest of the family arrived by Friday. The house was full and that kept us busy too. Fortunately, several months before our mother died, she had already decided on what she wanted to wear for her funeral and gave me the saree and everything that went with it for her burial. Accompanied by Kumila, I went to the funeral parlor early Friday morning. The folks at the funeral parlor did not know how to put an Indian saree on mother. I had helped our mother several times before, but this was different. She was no longer alive. Her body was cold. This was an awesome privilege, but it took a lot of courage. Thankfully, I was so numb that I did not feel any emotion as I performed this final task. Fortunately, I was able to dress my mother and she lay there looking beautiful in her Sunday best. Strangely enough, the pain, suffering, and being away from her loved ones had not left their mark on her. She looked beautiful as ever taking a well deserved nap free from suffering, with a smile on her face as if she was glad to be with her Maker and our loved ones who had gone before. The service at the funeral parlor was a big surprise for us. Mother knew very few people who actually communicated with her so our expectation was for a very low attendance. But word had spread to all our friends including the parents of past and present students, coworkers, and neighbors who all attended the service. It was very moving to hear how our mother had touched their lives.

On Saturday after the burial at the cemetery we attended the Praise Service at the church. It was a service where our mother's children and grandchildren participated. Again, even though only a few church members actually knew our mother, the service was well attended. It was a time when we praised God for the life our mother had lived and the legacy she had left behind. The church members surprised us with a wonderful spread at the reception to which everyone was invited.

The final celebration was over. In time the family would go back to their homes and Rajini and I would return to our home where the presence of the one who had played such a vital part in our lives would not be there. However, her memory would be embedded in our hearts and her faith in the living, loving God would encourage us to follow the examples left behind by both our parents. Indeed we were very fortunate to have parents like ours.

We thanked God for our parents and their love for God, their children, grandchildren, and great grandchildren. We have been fortunate to have had parents who with their instructions and their example, not only touched our lives but also the lives of those they came in contact with. They gave us the greatest gift. A gift no amount of money can ever buy and one the world can never give. They gave us an example of a life completely dedicated to a God who is the giver of every perfect gift. We are blessed and we hope and pray we can carry on the legacy they have left behind. I am sure they would love that.

PASSING THE BATON

One good thing about having children who are brought up in the ways of the Lord through example and precepts is the joy of knowing that the children can begin their adult life knowing how to depend on the Lord. The children are blessed because their parents had not only worked hard to follow in the ways of the Lord but took the time to help their children do the same. John and Bhagyabati Patnaik, from the very start, recognized the Creator God as the one who was not only the head of their home but the one who directed every step they took for themselves and for their family. As a result, God was able to do extraordinary things not only for them but for their children who were determined to walk in the ways of the Lord. We were fortunate to be the ones who benefited from having such parents.

Apart from the gift of salvation, having parents like ours was also a precious gift we were privileged to have. It was a God-given gift and we were the proud recipients. And now even though my sister Umie and I are single and have no children, God expects us to pass the baton on. So, it is our hope and desire that you, the reader, will benefit from what we learned as my parents not only modeled it and taught it to us but passed the baton to us. I hope you in turn will not only benefit from it but pass it on too.

What made my parents remarkable?

It wasn't because they were wise, learned people who always made the right choices at the right time. The Bible clearly states that we were born in sin and there is nothing good in us. In fact, "All our righteousness are as filthy rags." So, what was it that made our parents who they were? There were several things they did that brought them the results they hoped for.

The blue-collared people considered my parents to be less than ordinary people with very little skill and no qualifications. This was true. The good thing was that my parents saw themselves the same way and completely depended on the Lord their Savior for wisdom. They recognized the Creator God who not only created them but had the power to mold them to be the kind of vessel that He could use to bring glory to Himself. They had no one to introduce them to this Creator God, but they had His written Word. They read this Word with diligence and discovered that Jesus who was born in a manger and lived among men was God's only begotten Son.

This same Jesus taught us the way to eternal life and eventually gave His life to redeem man. As a result, they individually accepted Jesus as their Savior and Lord. Life without Jesus is worth nothing. He is the Master Teacher and was able to lead and guide my parents. My parents did not know how to raise children in the precepts of our Lord, but with Jesus as the Master Teacher and their dependence on Him enabled my parents to bring us up in the ways of the Lord.

Seeing how Jesus transformed their lives and used them for not only their family but those around them, caused us to accept this same Jesus as our Lord and Savior. We learned from a very early age to give our lives to Jesus and allow Him to lead and guide us through life's journey

They recognized the Bible as the written word of God; they took the time to read it diligently for themselves and made it an integral part of our family devotion every night. What a foundation they laid in our lives at a very young age! A foundation that was built on solid rock. A foundation that helped me to appreciate God's word and study it for myself as a daily prerequisite at the beginning of each day. I think for me, that was one of the greatest gifts and examples I received from my parents. It was something that was there for me even when they had departed, and I suffered the pain and emotional strain that came with it. It was the reading of God's Word that set the tone for the days that lay ahead of me.

It was also from my parents that I learned to talk with God as if He was someone who was right there waiting to hear his child. Having an earthly father who was prepared to listen to me after a hard day's work convinced me while I was still young that I could have that same relationship with my Heavenly Father. The only difference was that my Heavenly Father was available 24/7 from the time I was born until I leave my earthly home. He is right there in my joys and in my sorrows. He knows my needs even before I ask Him for help, and like a good loving father, He meets my needs in a way that is best and sufficient for me.

Raising seven children was not easy. But I noticed two things in my parents' life which seemed to give the impression that it was very easy.

The first thing I noticed was that my parents not only loved each other but respected each other. What is so unusual about that? In those days in India, there was no such thing as marrying for love. While a girl was still in her teens, a marriage was arranged for her by her parents. The young girl was made to understand she was fortunate to have someone who wanted to marry her and as such she should be content to get married. So, with this understanding, the bride entered the new home with the presumption that she was required to take care of not only her husband but the household duties and her husband's entire family and their own children. But since both my parents loved the Lord, even though my mother had to take care of the entire family, my father respected her and treated her with love and tenderness.

He taught us that when he was at work my mother was in charge and she would use her discretion in making the decisions during the day and we would have to respect those decisions and act accordingly. He would never listen to any complaints regarding what our mother said and did. I am sure there were many occasions when one of my parents disagreed with the other, but that was discussed in private.

They always had a united front where the children were concerned. That made us love and respect both parents and people in authority. This was important because we children learned from an early age that we could not use one parent against another.

Contrary to how people thought those days, our father made it clear to us that our mother was not a servant who had to do all the housework all day. He made Patricia and I understand that when we came home and had finished our school assignments, we had to clean up the house and scrub the utensils so that Mother could take a break like we did. Besides, he always reminded us that even when we started to earn a living we had to learn to make "a house a home."

He told us a house was a building but a home was a dwelling place for a family that loved and cared for each other. So, when we were home during our vacation, we had to learn how to cook and clean and take care of the house. At that time, we thought it was unfair, but when we became adults, we were glad we had been taught this important skill. No matter what our earnings were, we were always able to put food on the table after a hard day's work even when times or situations were difficult. The house had to be clean, neat, and tidy.

Through their example they taught us a work ethic. They believed in the "Dignity of Labor." It did not matter what we were asked to do or where we were placed to do a job; how we did it was what mattered. Father always reminded us that hard work killed no one.

With determination, desire, and God's help, we could do anything that was age appropriate. We had to first pay careful attention to the instructions given and then give the assignment our best shot. There was no harm in asking for help but no room for making excuses. It was important to feel that we had done our best at the end of a task. There was no shame in being a cook if that is what the Lord had called us to do. We had to be the best cook available. I think that principle is what made our father the best cook in his days and our mother the best (in our opinion) homemaker and a mother to be proud of. Dad was able to make the best Western and Indian food and please everyone he cooked for, and did it with a smile.

Dad taught us the importance of punctuality and to do everything with all our hearts. Though he worked almost eleven hours a day, he was always on time and never once complained even when he stood all day and cooked with a very bad knee. We had to remember that ultimately as believers, we were working for the "King of Kings" and we needed to give Him our best and hear His well done.

Through their example, they taught us to aim high. Though they came from a background where education was not a priority, they were determined with the help of God to send each of their children to schools that were meant for only those who could afford it. Because of their faith in God and their determination, we were able to graduate from good schools that made it possible for us to get good jobs with a good future. We were the first and probably the only ones in our generation to not only attend English schools and colleges but to go abroad for further education and establish a home there.

This was unheard of but became available to us because our parents worked hard, had implicit trust in God, and set a high standard for us. This was so ingrained in us that each one of us worked hard, trusted God, and allowed Him to do what was thought impossible in each of our situations. I know that people who came in contact with us were surprised we had all purchased homes in a very short time of our arrival in a foreign land. Each of us started our adult life with very little, but with hard work and willingness to do our best, and a goal in mind, we were able not only to survive but have a good home and have food on the table even during difficult times.

Our parents taught us the value of money. Although their income was nothing to be proud of, they knew that money would go a long way if it was treated as a gift from God. I still remember, and I have mentioned it before, that my mother would never spend Dad's earnings as soon as he gave it to her. The first thing she did was to take it in her hand and ask the Lord to bless it and multiply it so that it could provide for the needs of the family. Then she made sure each one of us had our coins for Sunday offering. She saved a small portion for a rainy day and finally used the rest to provide for the necessities of the family and pay the bills.

In my mind, I thought this was ridiculous. That was not how it worked. But my parents knew that the Bible asked us to give the first fruits to God and He would supply all our needs. And they were right. We children never knew a day when we had to go without food. In fact, if I remember, we all had our four well-balanced meals and always dressed in our Sunday best for church. That was a very important principle we learned which has helped us as we established our homes. God always helped us to pay our bills on time and we always had food on the table. *"Give and it shall be given to you; good measure, pressed down and shaken together and running over."* Luke 6:38 was a very important lesson for us to learn.

They also taught us the difference between needs and wants. God has promised to provide for the needs we have for survival. The wants were there because we desired to have but could do without. I know this is a very important lesson to learn especially these days when one can have anything they desire without a penny in their pocket. Then face the consequence of sleepless nights because of the debts that pile up.

I am glad we learned this lesson before we arrived in America. We had never seen huge shopping centers where you could get everything under the sun. There were times when we looked at the people around us and saw the cars they drove, the clothes they wore and the restaurants they visited and wished we had the same. I am sure the longings were there, but since getting a house was a priority, we saved every penny we could so that with the help of God we could buy a house within the first five years of our arrival in America.

We had learned the difference between a house and a home. In order to make that house a home for us, we learned from our mother how to save and improve on it. The result was a beautiful three-bedroom home with a master suite, a second bathroom, an open concept kitchen, a furnished den, an enclosed deck and beautiful gardens in the back and front. The result of this transformation allowed us to sell our home for top dollars, which enabled us to retire in comfort.

Getting to really know the people around us and being able to treat them as part of God's creation was a very important part in the lives of our parents which became a part of our lives. We grew up at a time when in India, groups of people were separated by religious ideology, occupation, and their status in life. It was quite usual to have one group of people think they were far superior to the next. They were also distinctly separated by the way they dressed, the language they spoke, and food they were allowed to eat and not eat. This caused great dissension among the people and made it difficult to move around. In fact, the percentage of Christians was less than 2% when we left India. We were a minority. Added to that the caste system in Hinduism created a great schism between the four caste groups. The Sudras were the lowest caste and were a group by themselves. They were the "Untouchables."

It was amazing to see how our parents not only got along with people of every group in the society but treated each one of them as friends and people created by God. They mingled with everyone unless they were criminals. My parents helped them understand we were all created by the one and only creator God. So, although we looked different and had different beliefs, we could live like brothers and sisters. We needed each other because no man was an island. Our home was open to all even if our mother had to cook food that was suitable for that particular group.

They taught us that hospitality was expected of us as believers and we were expected to greet and entertain anyone who took the time to walk through our doors. Although there were many fights between these groups, we were safe and accepted by all. In other words we were taught to be peacemakers. We were taught to respect their beliefs and celebrate Christmas with all, even those who were not Christians.

In times of difficulties or need, my parents were always there for our neighbors who knew my parents were available should they need help. We learned to share our food, our home, and even our time so we could set an example to the people around us. My parents were not preachers, but they lived a life which exemplified Christ and which caused others to seek guidance from them. In their simple way, they taught us how to live according to the precepts of our Lord and the teachings in the Bible which is the word of God.

From our early years, we had learned to respect the neighbors and their beliefs even though they were different and not according to the principals and beliefs of what we considered was according to God. In that way we were able to break barriers and have conversations without being dogmatic. We learned to live with others because they too were created by God to enjoy this beautiful world.

Now, as we have taken the baton from our parents, we are expected to live for Christ and share the teachings of Christ with those who live around us. We are only human and make many mistakes, but the Lord helps us in our inadequacies. Rajini and I do not have children to pass the baton to, but hope that through our lifestyle and our conversations, we have projected Christ in the places we worked and lived. I have been a teacher for 53 years and hope I was able to pass some of these learned lessons to the children that God placed in my care.

I do hope that like our parents we will be able to face our maker and hear His "Well done my good and faithful servant, enter into the joys of the Lord." Life goes on, but how we live our lives will either draw the ones we come into contact with to the Lord or drive them further to condemnation. We are a privileged people if we are born into the family of God. Let us then not only accept the baton passed to us but put in time and effort and allow the grace of God to help us pass it on to those around us. If you have children, introduce them to Christ and show them how to live for Christ by example. Teach them to make Christ the center of their lives. Then you not only pass the baton to the next generation but you have given the gift that will continue to grow when they give it to their children and to their neighbors and friends.

When the pilgrims first came to America, they left everything because they wanted the freedom to worship God. They did not have material possession, but they had Almighty God. They wanted to build an America on biblical foundation and we have the blessing of knowing and worshiping God freely, but for how long? We do have a responsibility that needs to be taken seriously. We cannot keep it to ourselves. We need to study the Bible, pray diligently, live it boldly, and "pass the baton" to the next generation.

"And the peace of God, which passeth all understanding will keep our hearts and minds through Christ Jesus" (Phillippians 4:7).

To God be the Glory for the things he has done.

Patricia, Rajini and Sushila with Zacheria

The Three Sons, The Wives, The Children and the 4 Grandchildren, Kumila and her
husband, Patricia and Stuart, Rajini and Sushila

Celebrating the Anniversary of Bis and Kumila

To My Readers

May I ask a very important question? Do you know my Jesus, and do you have a personal relationship with Him? He created each one of us with a purpose. His desire is that we glorify Him in all we do. He is the only way, the truth and the life. He is able to take us through every situation we face in life, but we must first accept Him as the Lord and Savior of our life. He will give us the peace that passes all understanding. It is peace that the world cannot give and can't take away.

There is a void in all of us until the Lord is allowed to fill it. He will give us a purpose in life and joy even when we are going through difficult situations.

Will you accept this free gift from Him? The word of God says, "Call on Him and He will answer". Say a simple prayer and give your life to Him. He will immediately accept you. Daily communicate with Him in prayer, read His word and ask Him to direct your life. Make sure you get together with fellow believers.

The word of God says in Luke 9:25, "For what is the man advantaged if gains the whole world and loses His soul" So my friend, submit to Him and see what He does in and through you. God bless you as you take this journey with Him.

www.ingramcontent.com/pod-product-compliance
Lightning Source LLC
Chambersburg PA
CBHW051209120626
46547CB00013B/1267